FRANCE

Marivaux

(TWAS 294)

TWAYNE'S WORLD AUTHORS SERIES (TWAS)

The purpose of TWAS is to survey the major writers—novelists, dramatists, historians, poets, philosophers, and critics—of the nations of the world. Among the national literatures covered are those of Australia, Canada, China, Eastern Europe, France, Germany, Greece, India, Italy, Japan, Latin America, the Netherlands, New Zealand, Poland, Russia, Scandinavia, Spain, and the African nations, as well as Hebrew, Yiddish, and Latin Classical literatures. This survey is complemented by Twayne's United States Authors Series and English Authors Series.

The intent of each volume in these series is to present a critical-analytical study of the works of the writer; to include biographical and historical material that may be necessary for understanding, appreciation, and critical appraisal of the writer; and to present all material in clear, concise English—but not to vitiate the scholarly content of the work by doing so.

To
Gunilla

Library of Congress Cataloging in Publication Data

Haac, Oscar A
    Marivaux.

(Twayne's world authors series, TWAS 294. France)
Bibliography: p.
1. Marivaux, Pierre Carlet de Chamblain de,
1688-1763.
PQ2003.Z5H3   842'.5   73-17338
ISBN 0-8057-2593-8

Marivaux

By OSCAR A. HAAC

State University of New York at Stony Brook

Twayne Publishers, Inc.   ::   New York

MARIVAUX

Preface

This book is the conclusion of long and extended studies in Marivaux; the articles resulting from investigations of various special apsects are listed in our bibliography. They pursue subjects further than has been possible here and are not incorporated as such. We are greatly indebted to the scholars listed in the bibliography. The reader will want to compare our interpretation with theirs, especially the useful discussion of texts, and analysis of criticism by E. J. H. Greene, and the editions and commentary of Frédéric Deloffre that have enabled us to present Marivaux so concisely and pertinently; his personal suggestions have been invaluable. This applies also to the stimulation received from a number of outstanding contributions, such as the Georges Poulet–Leo Spitzer debate, the suggestions of the *double registre* of Jean Rousset, or the revelation of new documents by Marie-Jeanne Durry, Giovanni Bonaccorso, Mario Matucci, and Michel Gilot, who enable us to interpret the background of Marivaux.

Ever so many acknowledgments of help received are in order, and personal thanks to those who discussed many topics with us, particularly also to Kay Wilkins whose suggestions greatly improved the manuscript.

Contents

Chronology

Dates are those of publication or first performance, cf. the Deloffre list in OD vii-xiii; T.F.= Théâtre Français Comédie Française; T.I.= Théâtre Italien, Italian troupe. For other abbreviations see the Bibliography.

1688 Feb. 4: Pierre Carlet is born in Paris to Nicholas Carlet and Marie-Anne Bullet, married in 1682.

1698 Dec. 31: Nicholas Carlet is appointed to the mint in Riom which he directs until his death in 1719. The family soon moves to Riom.

1710 Nov. 30: Pierre Carlet registers for the first time at the Faculty of Law in Paris. He does so again in 1711, 1712, 1713, and in 1721 when he obtains his degree.

1712 March - April: *Le Père Prudent et Equitablè* (comedy), performed in Sens and published with a preface signed M ***, the first indication of the name, Marivaux.

1713 *Les Effets Surprenants de la Sympathie,* Pts. I-III; Pts. IV-V follow in 1714 (novel). *Pharsamon* (burlesque novel), see 1737. *La Voiture Embourbée* (realistic short novel with an oriental tale).

1714 *Le Télémaque Travesti* (burlesque novel), see 1736. *Bilboquet* (brief satire in prose).

1716 Dec.: *L'Iliade Travestie* (mock epic in verse, 12 books). The dedication is signed "Marivaux"; it is the first time the name is given in full.

1717 July: Marriage to Colombe Bollogne, born Jan. 2, 1683, 5 years his elder. Sept.: *Lettres sur les Habitants de Paris* (essays in the *Mercure;* installments to Aug., 1718).

1719 April: *Pensées sur Différents Sujets* (essays in the *Mercure*). April 14: Death of Nicolas Carlet in Riom. Same period: Birth of Colombe-Prospère, Marivaux' daughter. Dec. *Lettres Contenant une Aventure* (essay in the *Mercure;* installments to April, 1720).

1720	March 3: *L'Amour et la Vérité,* in collaboration with Saint-Jory (comedy, T.I.), partly lost. Oct. 17: *Arlequin Poli par l'Amour* (comedy, T.I.). Dec. 16: *Annibal* (tragedy, T.F.).
1721	June 20: Marivaux obtains the Master of Laws *(licence).* July-Sept., 1724: *Le Spectateur Français* (periodical).
1722	May 3: *La Surprise de L'Amour* (comedy, T.I.).
1723	April 6: *La Double Inconstance* (comedy, T.I.). End or 1724? Death of Marivaux' wife.
1724	Feb. 5: *Le Prince Travesti* (comedy, T.I.). July 8: *La Fausse Suivante* (comedy, T.I.). Dec. 2: *Le Dénouement Imprévu* (comedy, T.F.).
1725	March 5: *L'Ile des Esclaves* (comedy, T.I.). Aug. 19: *L'Héritier du Village* (comedy, T.I.).
1726?	*Mahomet Second* fragment (tragedy) in the *Mercure,* March, 1747.
1727	Sept. 11: *L'Ile de la Raison* (comedy, T.F.). Dec. 31 *La (Seconde) Surprise de l'Amour* (comedy, T.F.).
1728	April 22: *Le Triomphe de Plutus* (comedy, T.I.).
1729	June 18: *La Nouvelle Colonie* (comedy, T.I. lost).
1730	Jan. 23: *Le Jeu de l'Amour et du Hasard* (comedy, T. I.).
1731	Spring: *La Vie de Marianne,* Pt. I (novel). Nov. 5: *La Réunion des Amours* (comedy, T.I.).
1732	March 12: *Le Triomphe de l'Amour* (comedy, T.I.). June 8: *Les Serments Indiscrets* (comedy, T.F.). July 25: *L'Ecole des Mères* (comedy, T.I.).
1733	June 6: *L'Heureux Stratagème* (comedy, T.I.).
1734	Jan.-April: *Le Cabinet du Philosophe* (periodical). End Jan.: *La Vie de Marianne,* Pt. II. April-April, 1735: *Le Paysan Parvenu,* Pts. I-V (novel). Aug. 16: *La Méprise* (comedy, T.I.). Nov. 6: *Le Petit-Maître Corrigé* (comedy, T. F.).
1735	May 9: *La Mère Confidente* (comedy, T.I.). Nov.: *La Vie de Marianne,* Pt. III.
1736	Feb.-Nov.: *Le Télémaque Travesti,* written 1714; anonymously published in Holland (burlesque novel). March-Nov.: *La Vie de Marianne,* Pts. IV-VI.
1737	Jan.-June: *Pharsamon,* written 1712-13, anonymously published (burlesque novel). Feb.: *La Vie de Marianne,* Pt. VII. March 16: *Les Fausses Confidences* (comedy, T.I.).
1738	Jan.: *La Vie de Marianne,* Pt. VIII. July 7: *La Joie Imprévue* (comedy, T.I.).

1739   Jan. 13: *Les Sincères* (comedy, T.I.).

1740   Nov. 19: *L'Epreuve* (comedy, T.I.).

1741   *La Commère* (comedy for T.I., not performed).

1742   March: *La Vie de Marianne*, Pts. IX-XI (end).

1743   Feb. 4: Marivaux is received into the French Academy.

1744   April: Marivaux moves into the apartment of Mademoiselle de
       Saint-Jean, rue de Saint-Honoré; they will make a financial
       agreement in 1757, move to rue Richelieu, and remain together
       until Marivaux' death. Aug. 25: *Réflexions sur le Progrès de
       l'Esprit Humain, sur Thucydide*, published in the *Mercure*, 1755
       (address to the Academy). Oct. 19: *La Dispute* (comedy, T.F.).
       Dec. 29: *Réflexions sur Différentes Sortes de Gloire* (lost
       address to the Academy).

1745   April: Colombe-Prospère becomes a novice at the Abbaye du
       Trésor at Bus Saint-Rémy (Eure) where she will take vows (end
       of 1746) and die (1788).

1746   Aug. 6: *Le Préjugé Vaincu* (comedy, T.F.).

1748   April 4: *Réflexions sur l'Esprit Humain*, perhaps incorporated
       into *Le Miroir*, 1755 (lost address to the Academy).

1749   Aug. 24, Sept. 24, Aug. 25, 1750: *Réflexions sur L'Esprit
       Humain à l'Occasion de Corneille et de Racine*, in part
       published in the *Mercure* 1755, 1757 (address to the Academy).

1750   Dec.: *La Colonie*, published in the *Mercure* (comedy for a
       private stage). Dec. 27-Jan. 8, 1751: As Chancellor of the
       French Academy, Marivaux pronounces official tributes.

1751   Aug. 24: *Réflexions sur les Romains et les Anciens Perses*,
       published in the *Mercure* (address to the Academy).

1755   Jan.: *L'Education d'un Prince*, published in the *Mercure* Dec.,
       1754, II (dialogue honoring the birth of Louis XVI). May 12:
       Unsuccessful address to the Academy, lost. Aug. 24: *La Femme
       Fidèle* (comedy for the Théâtre de Berny, partly lost).

1757   March 5: *Félicie*, published in the *Mercure* (comedy for the
       T.F.). *L'Amante Frivole* (comedy for the T.F., lost). Nov.: *Les
       Acteurs de Bonne Foi*, published in the *Conservateur* (comedy).

1761   *La Provinciale*, published anonymously in the *Mercure*
       (comedy).

1763   Feb. 12: After prolonged illness—his testament is dated Jan. 20,
       1758—Marivaux dies in rue Richelieu.

CHAPTER 1

Introduction

MARIVAUX remains the author perennially unknown even though, in France at least, he has become a classic widely read, performed, and discussed. His plays are produced more frequently on the French stage than any others beside those of Molière; his novels are frequently reedited; his essays and miscellaneous writings have received attention. The problem is Marivaux' reticence to reveal himself. He hardly ever speaks as the author. Even when we discover episodes with autobiographical elements, we must be on our guard; even when he pleads for complete sincerity, he is wearing a mask. Marivaux left almost no correspondence (only three letters and three brief notes are extant) and does not speak of himself. As a result, even the most elementary facts of his biography, the names of his parents, the dates of the birth and death of his wife and his daughter, have been established only quite recently from legal documents. The only record of his childhood is what can be inferred from official reports of the royal mint which his father directed. In a way, this is an advantage, for critics are forced to devote themselves to his work which is, after all, what creates our interest. We shall attempt to discover the man through analysis of his writings. We also hope to stimulate the interest they deserve, for they are essentially unavailable in English. There are few translations; those that exist are often inadequate, and insufficiently represented in the popular anthologies of the theater. It is ironical that *La Vie de Marianne,* accurately translated into English in the 1740's and edited by Davis in London, thus known to Samuel Richardson who set type for Davis, has long gone out of print, while a fanciful adaptation by Mrs. Collyer has been reedited. We need accurate modern renditions of Marivaux' works; we hope that this study will stir translators to filling the gap.

It is a paradox to speak of Marivaux as a Classic, for he began his career as a fashionable iconoclast favoring the "Moderns" in the famous "Battle of the Books," maintaining that contemporary literature was more pertinent than the Classics of Greece and Rome that were taught in the schools. His friends and he accused the "Ancients" of worshiping the consecrated authors of the past only in order to deny the merit of their contemporaries. Marivaux wrote in the spirit of revolt against what was considered "Classic" in his day, i.e., judged valuable enough to be taught in the classes of rhetoric, the only place in the curriculum where literature was discussed at all. These classes attempted to make young Frenchmen into little Ciceros. The closer they followed Cicero and Quintilian, the better. Such was the opinion of Rollin who loved his Classics and, as the superior teacher he was, had written the most popular manual to guide the teachers of his day.

In rebelling against Rollin and the accepted standards of style, in associating with Fontenelle and especially La Motte who spoke for the "Moderns" in the salon of Madame de Lambert, Marivaux shocked critics of the traditional mold, like Desfontaines, and provided ammunition to contemporaries jealous of his fame, themselves Classicists who, like Voltaire, set out to denigrate Marivaux' "metaphysics of love." Their criticism did much to injure Marivaux' reputation. He had to wait longer than Stendhal to be generally accepted. It was only quite recently that the *Petit Larousse* revised the definition of *marivaudage* from "precious and exaggerated speech like that of Marivaux" to read: "refined and precious speech like that of Marivaux," and even this formulation is neither complimentary nor adequate, for it overlooks his realism, the comic imitation of refined manners on the part of servants who never succeed in mastering them, the ambiguity of human motives ever present even in refined speech which barely covers up greed and sensuous desire.

What seemed so objectionable was Marivaux' style, first of all his syntax and use of language, then, by implication, the use to which it was put, the form of plays and novels, the radical break with tradition. Desfontaines attacked Marivaux' stylistic expression but also what he judged to be inappropriate to the form or genre, language inappropriate to comedy or a novel that did not progress and develop its plot. Today Marivaux seems to be a purist, the creator of Classical style, the continuator of the seventeenth-century tradition, but in his day his impact was very different. After all, comedy, for over a century, had been a form of satire of man's foibles written in alexandrine twelve-syllable verse. It was unusual to adopt prose for comedies of character. Tragedy had been devoted to the portrayal of noble heroes pitted against fate. When Marivaux writes a tragedy where the heroes suggest reasonable compromise, or comedies which involve noble sentiment, he challenges the accepted mold.

He continues the analysis of motives in the tradition of French *moralistes,* but combines idealism and the realistic appraisal of the ambiguity of human motives. The Classicists of his day could not accept the study of serious motives for comic effect, the application of what seemed to be philosophical techniques to perfectly common emotions, the lack of concern for abstractions that were held in high honor, the principles for which the heroes of French Classical tragedy were willing to die, now reduced to elements of comedy. On the public stage at least, Voltaire clung to the didactic function of literature while Marivaux seemed to toy with it. His style is often popular, naïvely simple, i.e., burlesque. Grand principles, essentially misunderstood, are uttered by servants or peasants who, in other respects, are their masters' alter egos, servants who are frequently more sensible than their masters in spite of their droll expressions.

Thus Marivaux created new genres not only for the stage, but in the novel which, traditionally, had concentrated on plot and featured fated passion. He reduced the element of plot; he left novels incomplete when it bored him to write the obvious conclusion; he used elements of popular speech which, as everyone believed, should be heard but not seen in print and which had been banned from the refined spirit of salon society, reflected in literature.

So it was that the first favorable interpretation of his work appeared no less than 130 years after his death, Larroumet's thesis of 1893. Another fifty years were needed until truly remarkable performances changed the image of Marivaux. In 1946, Jean-Louis Barrault presented *Les Fausses Confidences,* in 1950, *La Double Inconstance* was staged by the Comédie Française, in 1956, *Le Triomphe de l'Amour* by Jean Vilar and the Théâtre National Populaire. Planchon's *Seconde Surprise de l'Amour,* in 1959, was noted for the sensual overtones which may have been overdone but had too long been overlooked. Plays that had hardly ever been produced, like *L'Ile de la Raison* and *Félicie,* proved surprisingly successful when performed by L'Equipe between 1950 and 1958. As to the novels, one famous episode did much to bring them to public attention, Gide's listing *La Vie de Marianne* as one of the ten best of French literature; at the time he had not even read it!

Marivaux' battles with critics produced essays in which he sharply reacted against what he considered unjust and abusive attacks. In so doing he formulated a theory of literature which is as original as his creative work. At times he became so deeply annoyed that he interrupted publication, but he also returned to the fray. His opinions illuminate his personality, as does his manner of stating them. He is a conscious artist who takes his role very seriously. A deep and humanitarian concern hides behind the comic facade, but he lets nothing distract him from his major objective, which is to amuse the reader, or spectator, to flatter him by making him understand the characters better than they understand themselves. Comedy becomes an effective technique for analysis, a "science of the human heart." Marivaux is an intelligent observer of society, a superb artist of language, who prefers to imply rather than emphasize, and lets his characters speak for themselves.

We shall discuss his work and opinions in chronological order, and follow his evolution from his first imitative enterprises to the works that develop an independent style, his refined and forthright analysis, sensitive and realistic at the same time. We shall summarize plots but concentrate on interpretation. Then, in chapter seven of our study, we shall review his technique, his style, his literary art, and, finally, survey a number of themes that can be followed through his entire work. Our investigation could have been undertaken from the perspective of each of these, and other themes could have been sought out; they are suggestive of many future studies. Our final survey will help us understand why we read, and admire, Marivaux, and what he stands for. Marivaux speaks to us more pertinently and more clearly than to any generation since his own.

CHAPTER 2

The Early Years of Marivaux

PIERRE Carlet was born in Paris, on Feb. 4, 1688, to Nicolas Carlet, formerly a naval officer at Le Havre, about to become supply officer with the army in Germany (1688-97), and to Marie-Anne Bullet. Her brother, Pierre, was a well-known architect and a cousin, Jean-Baptiste Bullet de Chamblain, admitted to the Royal Academy of Architecture in 1699, so impressed the young boy that he used "de Chamblain" as part of his name for some time.

When his father became director of the royal mint in Riom (1698), the family moved to that small town in central France (near Clermont-Ferrand and Vichy). It has been found that most of the directors of mints were in severe financial difficulties at the time and accused of mismanagement for not being able to separate personal and State funds. Such was not the case of Nicolas Carlet, but his was a thankless task, full of friction with the personnel, poorly rewarded except for a large, somber apartment. Marivaux' father became frustrated and bitter; honest, honorable, he worked at his task until his death in 1719. Father figures in Marivaux' work are often drawn on his model, forthright and usually appealing personalities, often unable to understand their children, showing their sympathy the best way they know.

Pierre stayed at Riom even when he enrolled at the Faculty of Law in Paris, in 1710. He did not take up residence in the capital until two years later, about the time when he published his first play and adopted the name of Marivaux (first used in 1716, cf. chronology). He did complete his law degree nine years thereafter (1721) and, the following year, is listed as "a trial lawyer of Parliament," but he concentrated on making a name for himself as an author. Soon after his arrival in Paris he must have met Fontenelle, who gave the approval for the printing of his first novel (1713). Through Fontenelle the young man met men of letters, was able to join the salon of Madame de Lambert, and took up battle with the "Moderns" around (Houdar de) La Motte. There is a touching tribute to Madame de Lambert in *La Vie de Marianne* (in Pt.

[19]

IV of 1736; she had died in 1733) and another to Madame de Tencin whose salon he joined later and who organized his election to the French Academy in 1742.

Salon society helped Marivaux' career, but his progress is based on an intense effort. By 1715 he had written five novels and a brief satire, first adopting the tradition of tales of adventure, then parodying the genre. In 1716 he carried his predilection for burlesque parody too far by versifying the twelve long books of a mock-epic, *L'Iliade Travestie*, which was to support the cause of La Motte but came too late to be effective. He learned his lesson and, in 1717, began writing in the realistic style that became his distinguishing mark and brought him success. The analysis of motives became his primary intent; the acuity of his psychological analysis, based on minute distinctions, provoked the reproach of excessive refinement, *marivaudage*. We shall deal with this when discussing later works, e.g., *Les Serments Indiscrets*.

In 1717 he married Colombe Bollogne. The fact she was five years his elder appeared unusual enough to give rise to comment; jokes related to this recur frequently in his work. In 1719, their daughter, Colombe-Prospère, was born; in 1720, serious financial difficulties beset the family when he lost most of his wife's dowry, his only wealth, in John Law's Louisiana speculations. His wife died in 1723 (or 1724); no suitable marriage could be arranged for the daughter who, eventually, joined a convent in Normandy (1745).

The story of Marivaux is almost entirely the record of his work. It is surprising how little we know about him. We do have anecdotes like those reported by the abbé Trublet who knew him well but could not always understand him. The poor abbé, not the most brilliant of men, complains that Marivaux is touchy and refuses to give explanations when one asks him what he meant. There are also the comments of Lesbros de la Versane, often disappointingly imprecise, and the eulogy by d'Alembert, remarkable but, in many ways, failing to perceive Marivaux' merit as we see it today. There are the comments on the salons he frequented (Madame de Tencin died in 1749), the records of the Academy (he attended faithfully), but they do not reveal Marivaux, the man and author. The best we can do is to let him emerge from his work.

CHAPTER 3

The Works of Youth

I   Le Père Prudent et Equitable
(A Father, Prudent and Just),
comedy in 1 act in verse for an amateur stage in Limoges, 1712.

A "printer's notice" would have it that Marivaux wrote his first play very rapidly as a wager with friends, but we sense considerable effort in his alexandrine verse and in the adroit use of sources: Regnard's *Légataire Universel* furnished the idea of a crafty servant who helps his young master by various impersonations designed to deceive his father, including one role in female attire. Other scenes, and particularly the solution, stem from Molière; Cléandre wins a lawsuit and becomes wealthy, i.e., acceptable as a suitor for Philine's hand, for her father, Démocrite, vowed that she would not marry into poverty.

The play is weak, but there are indications of Marivaux' spirit and originality, for instance, in the use of paradox. Démocrite, the father, considers himself prudent and just for giving his daughter the choice of three husbands, but he happens to disregard her love for Cléandre. Démocrite is absolutely grotesque when he presents his three choices in order of financial advantage: first Ariste, who is not only wealthy but old enough to die soon; then Monsieur de la Boursignière, a banker; last, the Chevalier. Paradox also appears in the fact that Crispin's elaborate impersonations to discourage the three official suitors take up most of the action but become useless when uncovered. Cléandre wins out only because he becomes wealthy!

The emphasis on feeling is new. Philine follows the way of the heart; she resolutely opposes not only her father who thinks of money, but Cléandre who first wants her to violate her father's trust and elope with him (she loves her father too much for that!) and then suggests the "infallible way to obtain consent," pregnancy. "If my love is dear to me," she objects, "my virtue matters even more" (T I, 14-15). At this point Cléandre feels dejected:

> *Mon crime est d'avoir eu le coeur trop enflammé;*
> *Vous m'aimeriez encor, si j'avais moins aimé.* (T. I, 16)
> (My crime flows from my heart in flame and stress;
> You still would love me had I but loved you less.)

This is the tone of Classical tragedy. The poetry is much more adequate than has been conceded, and this applies equally to comic passages like the following assertion of Démocrite:

> *En est-elle moins bien pour avoir un barbon?*
> *Non!* . . . (T I, 16)
> Would her fate be worse with a greybeard, though?
> No! . . .

The internal rhyme is appropriate and funny. The mixture of the tragic and the comic genres expresses Marivaux' new spirit. This is evident also in the servants' comments on their masters' love and anguish. Crispin speaks of "their pain and martyrdom." Toinette says: "Their sad and deathlike airs suit them well." Whereupon Crispin: "How wonderful to weep when one is in love" (T I, 17-18). Sentiment communicates itself to the servants, though their reactions are droll. Toinette begs Démocrite to be sensitive to Philine's love, but Cléandre, with his recent inheritance, is acceptable without such sentimentality (T I, 54).

The emphasis on feeling modifies Molière's concept of comedy. Intuitively Marivaux knows that he cannot surpass the master at his own game. D'Alembert comments in his *Eulogy:* "Unfortunately he did not esteem Molière and even more unfortunately he did not hide these feelings." We might say "fortunately" instead, for his distrust safegarded Marivaux' originality.

II   Les Effets Surprenants de La Sympathie
(The Surprising Results of Affection),
novel in 5 parts, I-II: 1713; III-V: 1714.

Clorante and Caliste are starry-eyed lovers. They pursue one another through horrendous dangers while Clorine, hopelessly in love with the hero, is unable to attract him. It is a long and complex tale written in the tradition of seventeenth-century romances from the *Astrée* to La Calprenède, Marivaux' immediate source of inspiration. Indeed, our author was so fascinated with his story, that he told it once again in *Pharsamon,* his next novel, undertaken about the same time, but now in the form of a parody. Once again he seeks distance from the models he follows. Progressively he becomes a critic, an interpreter rather than the chronicler of love and adventure.

The all-important preface *(Avis)* states that the novel is to move the reader. If it fulfills this purpose and touches ladies' hearts, it cannot be worthless (OJ, 5-6). Marivaux identifies Oreste, in Racine's *Andromaque,* as his model for "extraordinary terror" and "madness" that arouse compassion (OJ, 7). Corneille and Racine are frequently cited by him for their portrayal of passion and analysis of motives and he follows their precepts, be it in comedy or in the novel. Classical tragedy is his essential inspiration and he hopes that the reader who loves rules (Classical structure) will not be insensitive to this work which is less "regular" (OJ, 3-4). Clearly the mind *(esprit)* is at the service of the heart, though reason remains the all-important tool of analysis of what has happened. It provides *"réflexions"* which suspend the action and interpret its significance. Marivaux is proud, above all, of these reflections. A tale of pure adventure is soon discarded; the reflections lend it lasting value (OJ, 9).

The story, often told in the first person, is put into the mouths of different characters. Their accounts are interpolated into each other. At times it is difficult to know who is speaking. There is one moment when Caliste, under the assumed name Isis, is telling Clarice of her ancestors. She pretends that her father, Frédélingue, is telling his life; he in turn, has his wife, Parménie, tell her story; Parménie then listens to Merville, who consoles her with the tale of his own misfortunes; all these accounts are in the first person. Such is the traditional structure of the novel as practiced by La Calprenède. There results a deplorable confusion, an accumulation of unsurpassed passion and irrational acts of violence. Caliste's great-grandfather, Erisman, was as much of a madman as the wild suitors from whom her father, Frédélingue, rescued her mother, Parménie. Caliste herself is pursued by Périandre who listens only to his desires, while Clarice, the very image of despair, succumbs to Turcamène, when she has lost all hope of being loved by Clorante.

The most striking scenes are found in the last two parts, written in 1714. Two of these occur in the story of Merville. He tells how he has been abducted by pirates and enslaved in North Africa; his master's wife, as well as her maid, Frosie, are in love with him. "I shall tell my mistress you are coming to see her," says Frosie, "but what shall I tell myself?" (OJ, 220). In a remarkable exchange foreshadowing the art of dialogue in the plays, Frosie fears that love will make her more of a slave than Merville; he may regain his freedom and leave her. Soon thereafter, Merville finds the woman he really loves, Misrie, abused in a deep mine where slaves are being whipped by order of the mine owner, Ghirlane, who happens to be Misrie's mother and also her rival for the love of Merville (OJ, 227-30). The situation is grotesque but the description of the suffering slaves in the mine has an original tone. It adds a humanitarian motive which appears again when Frédélingue sets out to educate a group of island natives. He quickly eradicates superstition and convinces the savages of the value of legal marriage (OJ, 282-90). This is a utopia like Bétique in Fénélon's *Télémaque* or like that of Tyssot de Patot in his *Voyages de Jacques Massé*. Marivaux includes elements of social concern. Other episodes introduce a new realism into the novel: Turcamène, thinking he has poisoned his arch rival, will now subdue Clarice by force. His eyes shining, he shouts: "I would not have been as glad had she consented" (OJ, 85).

Many of the reflections, so important according to the preface, are less significant and subtle than those in later works. Some are commonplace indeed: "How rash lovers are!" (OJ, 55); "if you abhor crime, no evil man can tempt you!" (OJ, 82); when Clorante's father is forced to drink poison, he exclaims: "The innocent find help!" (OJ, 20). He does find an antidote though the reader does not know this for hundreds of pages (OJ, 302). Other reflections foreshadow the master. Blinded by his love for Caliste, Clorante leaves Clarice in the clutches of Turcamène: "How love weakens the virtue of a gentleman since its first test is also its last" (OJ, 89). If a "gentleman" like Clorante cannot aid a defenseless girl, what then of those who are not gentlemen? Numerous descriptions of murder and rape provide the answer. Most of *Les Effets* is given over to the "Romanesque," i.e., the extraordinary in the most traditional sense.

III   Pharsamon,
novel, 1713, publ. 1737.

La Calprenède had written a novel, *Pharamond;* Marivaux adopts its title with a pun on "farce," for this time he sets out to lampoon the genre. He recasts the story of *Les Effets* in the burlesque mode. Just as *Don Quixote* was a parody of novels of chivalry, just like so many other novels written in that style from Charles Sorel, *Le Berger Extravagant* (in imitation of Cervantes, similar in spirit to *Pharsamon,* but apparently unknown to Marivaux), to James Joyce, so *Pharsamon* made fun of *Les Effets* and all its precursors. Marivaux wants to gain critical distance through satire. *Le Don Quichotte Moderne* and *Les Nouvelles Folies Romanesques (The New Romanesque Follies)* were subtitles for *Pharsamon.*

The novel tells us that Pierre Bagnol, alias Pharsamon, as well as his beloved Cydalise, have read too many tales of fated love. Their minds are deranged and they seek each other through fanciful adventures until they are finally cured by a magician, like Cervantes' *Licenciado Vidriera*; whereupon they forget each other. Pierre Bagnol settles down with a well-preserved matron who made his recovery possible.

The best parts are the burlesque accounts by Cliton, the hero's Sancho Panza, hard drinking but with both feet on the ground, always willing to support and emulate Pharsamon (OJ, 506f, 526f); also Pharsamon's attack on a supposed castle as he brandishes a spit for a sword (OJ, 514-16). Let us also note a scene where a young student of law is making his way in society, much like the author (Oriante, OJ, 474f). The transposition into contemporary France of themes from Cervantes and the romances of the past is a major achievement. Marivaux combines elements of the burlesque novel of Sorel, Scarron, and Furetière with sentiment as found in the *Astrée,* or in Classical tragedy.

Pharsamon is far simpler in structure than *Les Effets*. It contains only two inserted episodes. Its complexity is of a different sort, created by the constant interplay of reality and fantasy. The element of realism gives rise to interesting and original descriptions. Even an apparently insignificant episode *(un rien)* can be worthier of our attention than a heroic deed and give the reader pleasure: two children and an apple provide a remarkable example (OJ, 562, 602). The theory is original but the result is no masterpiece. Marivaux was dissatisfied with the novel and in 1732 he planned to revise it. When it appeared in the original form, in 1737, he pretended it was not his own, for the burlesque tradition was disliked in the salons and in the society where Marivaux was making his career.

IV   La Voiture Embourbée
(The Stagecoach that Stuck in the Mud),
a short novel, 1714.

Before completing *Pharsamon,* Marivaux composed an imaginative and successful work. It consists of two parts. In the first, a group of travellers takes the stagecoach from Paris to Nemours. It breaks down. The dirt and poverty of a village inn are described. Dishes are so dirty that it seems preferable to drink water from a hat; the food cannot be touched. Eventually they negotiate a meal in the home of the local parson.

The second part is the tale they invent to pass the time while the stage is being repaired. The author who pictures himself as one of the travellers, initiates the story of "Famed Amandor and Beautiful, Intrepid Ariobarsane." The style at first is not unlike that of *Pharsamon;* The hero and the heroine are deluded by reading all too many novels of adventure and set out to realize their Romanesque dreams. However, as other travellers take turns inventing sequels to the story, the atmosphere changes; they each reveal their personality, their hopes and illusions.

First to take over the account is a lady with a passion for the *Arabian Nights* that had been appearing in the Galland translation since 1708. She associates the oriental spirit with old-fashioned ideals of chivalry and defends them in these terms:

Notions which inspire only virtue should not be considered foolish by anyone. Centuries past held them to be virtues because nobility and magnanimity were then as common among men as today self-interest, avarice, and sensuality. (OJ, 354)

What she fails to realize is that the episodes she tells to illustrate her philosophy prove precisely the opposite, for she speaks of a past of inhumanity and violence.

She lets Ariobarsane set out in male disguise, as a knight errant to right wrongs. She leads her to the cavern where Créor has been torturing his victims for centuries. Two hundred years before, she explains, Créor's fifteen-year-old sweetheart, Bastille, was carried off by the Sophi. Unable to resist the power of this prince, Créor grudgingly accepted a large gift of money in compensation, but secretly vowed a horrible vengeance. One day he happened to prevent a woman from killing a sleeping old man. He discovered that he had saved the life of a sorcerer who had the gift of eternal youth since he could enter the body of young men at will (he was so "delicate" as to choose victims who would soon die anyhow, OJ 336), but he could stay young only six days a week; the seventh day he reverted to his real age of two hundred and sixty years, and one of those days his woman slave tried to kill him. The sorcerer promised Créor that he would help him recover Bastille.

This is where the lady breaks off her tale. The story of Bastille will become the source of one of Marivaux' most famous plays, *La Double Inconstance*. The fantasy of rape and murder, which is said to be an evocation of virtues of old, proves not only the delusions of the lady traveller, but illustrates the spirit of outmoded traditionalists, of the "Ancients" who held up the Classics as models of style and virtue, without realizing that they glorified tales of man's inhumanity to man. Marivaux had joined the party of the "Moderns" and defended, as we shall see, a more humane and realistic attitude.

A young dilettante, posing as a wit and man of letters (*bel esprit,* cf. OD, 765), continues the plot. He tries to prove himself a man of the world by portraying atrocities without the slightest compunction. Créor kills the sorcerer to inherit his powers, and transports Bastille, the Sophi, and numerous other victims to his cave of horrors. A bewitched Bastille has perforated the Sophi with a dagger; for two hundred years the Sophi and other victims have been hanging, suspended in eternal torture, while Créor and his best friend abuse and kill scores of beautiful girls. The would-be wit is even more unrealistic and cruel than the lady whose account preceded his.

Now her attractive daughter takes over. She shows the maturity and common sense of the new generation. Her beauty may inspire romantic illusions, for the banker ogles at her all the time, but she does not share such attitudes: She simply ends the nightmare by waking Ariobarsane from a dream and sends her to a peasant home where, true to the story of *Au Clair de la Lune,* friend Pierrot is about to kiss the farmer's wife when her husband appears. A grotesque scuffle ensues. The bold peasant language and the everyday situation show that the girl knows the facts of life. She speaks like Cliton in *Pharsamon,* or like ever so many characters in the *Télémaque Travesti,* the novel Marivaux was soon to write in the mock-heroic manner. The girl who is talking is neither scared nor shocked at reality; she is an author such as Marivaux hoped to be.

There follows the elderly banker who had proven his professional talents by negotiating the meal from the Curé. His romantic dreams of love express themselves as he reunites Amandor and Ariobarsane.

The parson's nephew, neither brilliant nor subtle, is just the kind of person Marivaux feels would enjoy adding an obvious conclusion. He describes a drinking bout to celebrate the happy couple. The precipitation and irony of the end become characteristic of Marivaux, who will leave his major novels incomplete rather than convey the obvious.

New in *La Voiture Embourbée* is the great share of realism, not only in the setting, but implied in the psychology of the travellers whose stories reflect their own merits or shortcomings. Marivaux is well under way toward what Jean Rousset, in *Forme et Signification,* called his "double register," the contrast between what the characters say and what the reader understands.

Marivaux is frankly proud of his short novel. In a comic preface he makes fun of the fact that authors are not supposed to show their satisfaction; would they be publishing their work if they were not proud of it? Must he, to be in good taste, speak with hypocritical modesty? Thus Marivaux engages a dialogue with his critics, a dialogue which was often to become bitter but which forced him to state his position clearly and evolve a theory of literature.

V   Bilboquet,
a short parody, 1714;
Letter to a Lady, *1718*

A cup-and-ball game has become the rage of society; it is called *bilboquet.* Players are required to catch a wooden ball, provided with an appropriate hole, on top of a stick; the ball is attached by means of a string. Marivaux feels that this eighteenth-century Yo-Yo has become the lowest common denominator of conversation, an aberration as dangerous as the enthusiasm for the novels of adventure. In his brief fantasy, Bilboquet is the son of Folly and Ridicule. He makes Philis forget her lover!

In a somewhat similar satire, four years later, this time in the form of a poem with a few lines of prose, the *Letter to a Lady on the Death of her Parrot* (OD, 41-47, 1718), Marivaux again exercises his fantasy by mocking fantasy, for the lady lost touch with the world over her parrot. These are trifles, but also exercises in paradox characteristic of Marivaux' later style.

The most remarkable thing about *Bilboquet:* the only copy preserved was discovered recently by Professor Durry.

VI   Le Télémaque Travesti
(Telemachus, a Parody),
novel written 1714, published anonymously 1736.

Pharsamon had recast the adventures of *Les Effets Surprenants* into contemporary France for comic effect, as a parody of the old type of romance; in an analogous manner, Fénelon's didactic novel, *Télémaque,* set in ancient Greece while Telemachus was searching for his father, Ulysses, (it is intended to teach the art of government) is recast into the French provinces of around 1700. Marivaus follows Fénelon chapter by chapter, but for his own purposes; the parody is not directed against Fénelon, but against the conditions that are described. The novel is a superb document of popular wit and speech; its spirit is as different from its Classical model as possible.

Fénelon described contests of arms on Crete; Marivaux moves the scene to a French country fair where young Brideron earns many prizes and is named instructor in a local school. His mentor, Timante, adopts the Classical name of Phocion for comic effect; Calypso becomes Mélicerte; she well remembers Brideron's father whom she loved before he left for the Hungarian wars (he has not been heard of since and Brideron is looking for him as Telemachus was for Ulysses), and now she is furious that young Brideron prefers one of her maidens to her own mature charms.

The parallel to Fénelon's novel is exploited to the point where the characters, who have read it, seem to know what is about to happen. They are all the more surprised when, for once, their predictions are foiled: Fénelon's utopia, Bétique, has vanished from the earth. The pessimistic implications are evident, for Bétique had inspired Marivaux' account of a utopia near the end of *Les Effets Surprenants.*

The tone is one of skeptical realism. We find an impressive array of miscarriages of justice. Pymion is nothing but a petty tyrant. Omenée is a misguided ruler who trusts a villainous counsellor but dismisses his most faithful advisor, kills his wife, and now faces a peasant revolt for having not only ransacked Huguenot farms, but seduced the farmers' daughters. "They corrupt themselves," is his apology (OJ 835). Phocion and Brideron are able to arrange a grotesque peace. It calls for an extended drinking bout and stipulates that, henceforth, the farmers' daughters will be safe and that two weeks' warning will be given before legal pillaging in the name of king and religion. Episodes in the Camisard wars are recounted in similar, almost Rabelaisian style. The works of Rabelais were reedited that same year; Marivaux may have read them. By implication, the novel calls for peace and tolerance. Marivaux was not alone in feeling that the policies of Louis XIV had brought neither unity nor prosperity; he is original in condemning them on moral grounds.

The intent is serious; the tone remains droll. Fénelon's pedagogical purpose has been abandoned because Marivaux feels that literature cannot reform the reader. At one point we read: "It would be a mistake to tell you that you are a fool; princes don't want to hear such things" (OJ, 849). In lieu of moral principles we find humorous statements, gems of popular wisdom, pompous restatements of the obvious: "A wife may be quite faithful to her husband, but the uncertainty of it all! What a heavy burden!" (OJ, 723). "You can't lose by adopting the manners of a gentleman!" (OJ, 765). "What is dead is no longer alive!" (OJ, 771).

Fénelon died in 1715; his death may be related to Marivaux' reluctance to publish the novel, but there is a better explanation. He planned to rewrite it in the more traditional form of verse satire, as a mock epic. Arguments with the publisher and his next enterprise, a verse parody of the *Iliad,* explain initial delays. The failure of the parody of Homer was hardly an encouragement. Later on, the picturesque language of the *Télémaque Travesti* militated against publication. After the public outcry at the "low style" of a scene in his novel, *Marianne* (1734), where an argument between a laundress and a coachman shocked his readers, he was unwilling to see the *Télémaque* published; when it appeared against his will, in Holland, in 1736, he denied authorship. So few copies penetrated into France that half the work was presumed lost until resdiscovered by Professor Deloffre. It is unfortunate that Marivaux sacrificed so outstanding a piece in popular style to his career and his ambitions to enter the French Academy. The *Télémaque Travesti* is "literary" only in that no ordinary peasant could have expressed himself with such wealth of images and striking phrases; it is realism at its best.

VII   Homère Travesti ou l'Iliade en Vers Burlesques
(A Travesty of Homer or the Iliad in Burlesque Verse),
mock epic in 12 books, in verse, 1716.

Chapelain's *Pucelle* (1656, about Joan of Arc) and Scarron's *Virgile Travesti* (1648-67) consecrated the mock-epic as a Classical genre. Marivaux' more immediate model was the abbreviated version of the *Iliad* by his friend, La Motte, also in twelve books, in verse, an attack on war and Homer's unreasonable, self-centered heroes and vainglorious gods. A vigorous quarrel had arisen between La Motte and Madame Dacier, the translator and adamant defender of Homer. To support La Motte, Marivaux struggled hard to complete over four hundred pages of alexandrine verse; it took so long that the enemies had been officially reconciled by Valincour in the salon of Madame de Lambert. It is true that the issues that pitted "Moderns" against "Ancients" remained unresolved; Marivaux was to protest frequently against those who worshiped Classical authors only to denigrate the merit of their contemporaries and claim that none of their efforts could equal the glories of the past. Still, Marivaux is patently absurd. He admits never having read the original and says Homer must be worthless since he has inspired the virulent polemics of his translator. The humor of Marivaux' epic had definitely turned sour.

There are, even here, some passages of note. Marivaux appeals to common sense that should guide the reader in preference to the authority of Aristotle (X, 138), but then Aristotle's "authority" was a dead issue. Marivaux occasionally is funny, as when he explains that one modern physician is worth all of Homer's killers (X, 564), or when he comments in the style of the *Télémaque:* "Vanity makes chastity more difficult" (X, 210). There are a few happy images, as when a Trojan is compared to a caterpillar sticking to his position; worshipers of traditional rhetoric will prefer to speak of the Trojan "waves," we are told, for "success comes with big words" (X, 386-87).

All too often, however, the humor is heavy and platitudinous. Is it hilarious to find epic heroes upsetting a chamber pot? (X, 203) or reminiscing about the chickens they killed in ever so many villages? (X, 534) We read: "There is a country named France where being a cuckold is an advantage!" (X, 249). The humor is not unlike that of Voltaire, in his mock-epic, *La Pucelle,* where he comments on how difficult it was to find a virgin in France, when one was required to save the country. The *Homère Travesti* remains an exercise in shadow boxing, for Homer is not understood, the limitations of Madame Dacier do not concern the modern reader, and the description of Greek heroes like French country bumpkins was of little comfort to the "Moderns" even then. The work was an utter failure.

VIII   Lettres sur les Habitants de Paris
(Letters on the Residents of Paris),
essays published in the Mercure, *1717-18.*

The year Marivaux was married to Colombe Bollogne was also the year he discovered his true style, a happy coincidence. The essays on the Parisians of 1717 mark a great advance. The imitative phase of burlesque parodies is now ended. The essays inaugurate his long association with the *Mercure,* a periodical favorable to the "Moderns" that printed a number of his works and reviewed most of them. The technique of La Bruyère and the French *moralistes* prevails, even though Marivaux most vigorously protests against the nickname, "the modern Theophrastus" (OD, 22; La Bruyère translated Theophrastus). Marivaux prefers to be known as the continuator of the *Spectator* of Addison and Steele; translations had begun to appear in 1714.

He sets out to describe the classes of Paris society, first the common people, then the bourgeoisie, finally the nobility. His characterizations are original. The common people are qualified as impressionable, often violent, but without malice; like children, essentially good-natured but prone to use their fists; admirable in their sincerity. A thundering sermon may sway them but

I would advise no one to count on their religion, even of the most pious . . . . Their imagination is for the taking; replace one impression by another, replace the religious rite which made them pious with some proposition which appeals to their self-interest . . . . the latter will always win out . . . . Money is the only value they worship. The common people are like a large dog barking at all who pass by. (OD, 13-14)

One is more at ease with the bourgeois, a mixture of the popular and the aristocratic. The bourgeois mimics high society, but he is proud of his status. He can be friendly, even generous, but "don't touch his pocketbook!" We find a shopkeeper who talks a nobleman into buying cloth he does not need, then startles him by taking the money that is owed right out of the nobleman's purse. The nobleman, who had made a weak appeal to be allowed to leave without the merchandise, had imagined that the shopkeeper would be honor-bound to cancel the sale. The bourgeois have no such honor! (OD, 16). In his way, the merchant is honest; given a purse, he takes only what is owed; as Marivaux puts it: "One is both a merchant and a Christian" (OD, 17).

Like the nobleman, the bourgeois desires a mistress, only he expects wifely attentions from her (OD, 18). Pretty girls are, of course, always in danger, especially at the counter. They can easily find some elderly ruffian who provides money, and why not? After all, he pays for what he desires. "If this constitutes dishonor, all women would have to flee in shame!" One lady merchant keeps her lover close by the counter: "She may get away with it, but I don't think that her innocence does" (OD, 19).

When Marivaux turns to the lesser nobility, we sense how he identifies with his portraits. The small nobleman has only his title to make him proud. In his relations with bourgeois friends, he "finds compensation for the constraint he has suffered." In return, the bourgeois is flattered by his attentions and seeks his company. At times he glories in it like La Fontaine's frog who would blow himself up to be as large as an ox (OD, 25). "To acquiesce in one's estate is more admirable than being noble," but not all are capable of such a feat (OD, 23).

The ladies of society fascinate Marivaux. He devotes three entire pages to the negligee, "that conventional equivalent of nudity . . . that masterpiece of the desire to impress . . . of the art of being dressed without hiding anything, of revealing one's beauty without offending morals" (OD, 28). Ladies of society owe it to themselves to have lovers. It is their way of overcoming their strict upbringing, but isn't taking a lover also the first step in the ways of crime? (OD, 30) Of course everyone flirts, but there are strict limits. The "honorary coquette" flirts to prove she can be dissolute (OD, 31); the pious are not so different, for their assiduous visits to the confessional may show that love merely changed its name; "their soul deceives itself since it is never more worldly than when it seems to flee the world" (OD, 32).

Finally, Marivaux turns to the literary world. He ranks authors *(beaux esprits)* in a military hierarchy. Those who have published with merit are the generals; their staff officers are "the great mediocrities" capable of only the commonplace. Then follow the company grade officers, lucky to grasp a single idea; the most pedantic among them are the partisans of the "Ancients," translators who cling to outworn reputations, singing the praises of antiquity for lack of confidence, for fear of thinking independently; it is another attack on Madame Dacier (OD, 32-34).

When Marivaux turns to the tribulations of authors of superior intelligence, we feel that he describes his own anguish. Their readers understand them only in part though their analysis seems simple. Such authors shun cumbersome systems and treatises of philosophy, all that makes old-style philosophers so difficult—and esteemed. "Moderns" could express their observations as readily in a poem; they aim to be simple and appeal to sentiment.

The superior author has to contend with the reluctance of readers to recognize merit greater than their own; he must make his readers forgive his talent because of the pleasure they derive from it; he must practice his art without letting it show. Unless he can perform this feat, he is less superior than he may seem! (OD, 35-38).

Marivaux returns to the theme of the preface to *La Voiture Embourbée:* The author will feel proud of his work but must not seem too proud; he must avoid false humility and must impose himself without offending. One trick which enables the superior author to succeed is to praise his inferiors so that they will be inclined to praise him in return (OD, 39). This implies, at least outwardly, a spirit of conciliation like that which ruled the salon of Madame de Lambert; Marivaux will refrain from further attacks against the "Ancients" even though one was already announced (OD, 39, 42).

He was ill at ease facing his critics, but while countering their charges, formulated his theory of psychological analysis, his science of the human heart, as he was to call it later, outwardly facile and yet ever so serious and pertinent. He wants it to replace pedantic treatises which, by their very nature, were out-of-date and out-of-style. He yearns to be respected, like the modern scientists. We may resent his insistence on his intellectual superiority, but when we read the comments of the abbé Trublet (even though they concern a much later period), we come closer to appreciating his point of view (OD, 728-33); Marivaux was describing the lack of understanding he encountered in fairly objective terms! [1]

IX   Pensées sur Différents Sujets:
Sur la Clarté du Discours;
Sur le Sublime
(Thoughts on Sundry Topics:
On Clear Expression;
On the Sublime),
essays in the Mercure, *1719.*

To emphasize what he had said about the superior author, Marivaux added two essays the following year. He distinguishes between the perceptive mind *(esprit délicat)* and thick-heads *(esprit épais)* who cannot understand the author's meaning. Again we see Marivaux wrestling with the problem of communicating with his audience.

The constant charge, raised principally by the abbé Desfontaines, was that Marivaux' style was unclear. This charge gave rise to the first section concerning clarity. "To be clear, one need not have expressed all one has thought" (OD, 52), for "there is a degree of clarity beyond which ideas lose their force and precision" (OD, 54). Of course Marivaux admits that the author must be understandable; he must, above all, transmit his literary objectives; he must "express his ideas with the appropriate degree of forcefulness and meaning" (OD, 52). He must seek "the precise exposition of his thought as meaningfully and as truthfully as can be accomplished" (OD, 77). Marivaux turns to Classical tragedy, once again, to illustrate the point. When, in Corneille's *Horace,* Horace the elder condemns his son with the brief phrase: *Qu'il mourût!* ("Let him die," OD 56) he says a great deal, and clearly, in a few simple words.

Marivaux' requirements for an appropriate, expressive, but also analytical style that renders the implied feelings, is not unlike the proposal of the abbé du Bos who, in his *Réflexions Critiques sur la Poésie,* calls for terms which are "figurations of our ideas" (Pt. I, Sec. 33), or Malebranche who states: "Our understanding grasps the modifications of our soul or, rather, feels them, for by the term, 'understands,' I mean the passive faculty of the soul which conveys all the modifications of our experience." This passage stems from *La Recherche de la Vérité (The Search for Truth,*[2]), and this title could serve to sum up Marivaux' lifelong effort to uncover the nature of man and his feelings. Indeed, many parallels in Marivaux' essays point to the influence of Malebranche (cf. OD, index) and their kinship is not limited to adapting Descartes' rationalism and antischolastic attitude to social considerations, but extends to their common opposition of the "Ancients," and old-style philosophers. Malebranche devotes an ironical chapter in *La Recherche* to the "danger of reading," a danger to those "men of learning" (Marivaux calls them *philosophes*) who look for authorities to quote rather than think, who honor authors of antiquity so they can refuse their contemporaries any claim to greatness. Marivaux expresses these same feelings frequently and in almost identical terms. In the *Spectateur* he will introduce a character who trusts only ponderous tomes, certainly not the slender issues of Marivaux' periodical (OD 137-38). As "Moderns," Malebranche and Marivaux share a faith in man's intelligence, in his capacity to analyze his own complexity, and a passionate desire to understand man better. The aesthetics of du Bos and the philosophy of Malebranche impressed Marivaux and helped him develop his thought and literary style.

In this spirit, Marivaux defines the author's task: He must express the impressions of his soul sensitively and in appropriate style, with "sufficient clarity" but without an excess of detail that would destroy the unity or beauty of his account (OD, 54). Marivaux calls his critics' preoccupation with clarity "an obsession" *(une marotte)* which reflects more on their inability, or unwillingness, to grasp implications than on standards of good style (OD 55-56). Marivaux breaks with the platitudinous assumption that the essence of French literature is clarity, and shows that the tradition described by Daniel Mornet's *Histoire de la*

Clarté Française (History of French Clarity) is far less representative than Mornet assumed. The modern conception of style, as we find it in Marivaux, springs less from the idea of clarity than from the ideal of suggestive and subjective writing; it posits a style which is appropriate to its subject rather than conforming to standards of rhetoric.

There follows Marivaux' longer essay on the Sublime. The topic recalls Boileau's translation of Longinus, but is seen in a different perspective. Longinus dwelled on stylistic devices like apostrophe and periphrase (Chs. 14, 19-20, 24). Style, to Marivaux, is a function of sentiment (OD, 65); he distinguishes the Sublime in virtuous and guilty souls (OD, 61), in normal persons and those who are depressed and magnify even the smallest obstacle. He proposes that a single statement will strike readers differently depending on their frame of mind, just as the food at a banquet will be judged by each according to his own taste (OD, 68). One incident will cause witnesses to react differently (OD, 70). Here Marivaux returns to the distinction between the obtuse *(épais)* and the agile *(délicat)* minds; their reactions will vary greatly (OD, 70-71). Examples are again drawn from tragedy, from Crébillon and La Motte (we wish the illustrations were from greater authors!); it is no coincidence that Marivaux was writing his tragedy *Annibal* at the time. It is clear, however, that the theory applies equally to comedy, for there also Marivaux portrays the "anguished soul." In *La Surprise de l'Amour,* e.g., he pictures two lovers previously disappointed and, therefore, bound to entrap each other. Each play presents a particular, individualized situation, distinctions the common reader may miss, but which are essential and require an appropriate expression. Thus Marivaux departs from prescriptive rhetoric; he believes that each situation calls for its peculiar style and terms. His technique is one of psychological probing and analysis; his tool, a relativistic concept of style.

X   Cinq Lettres Contenant une Aventure
(Five Letters Containing an Adventure),
short story in the Mercure, *1719-20.*

The conversation between two girls, the social butterfly *(la folâtre)* and her sentimental friend *(la tendre),* is a small masterpiece of analysis and dialogue. The sentimental girl adores reading romances; presently she is desperate because the man she loves is off to visit his father. The coquette feels that she has more cause to grieve: her lover has gone to war. She wept helplessly when he departed, but by now she has gotten over this. She cultivates a number of rivals for his love. "My vanity is flattered," she admits. "I love him more when I can so easily be unfaithful" (OD, 78). After all, love needs to be stimulated by obstacles and competition. She recalls how her first suitor lost his ardor as soon as he obtained permission to visit her freely in the convent where she was then residing (OD, 81); he did not again become passionate until she had given him a number of rivals (OD, 89). Resistance strengthens love, satisfaction kills it (OD, 87). This theory recurs throughout Marivaux' work; he believed in it, and in the need for periodic "surprises of love" (OD, 89); we find them here for the first time. The coquette ends her account by telling how fortunate it was that, just as her lover's passion threatened her composure, one of his rivals arrived to disturb their rendezvous (OD, 100).

As part of her argument, she points out that we no longer live in the fairy world of seventeenth-century novels (OD, 75, 83-85, 91), where lovers swoon and remain faithful forever. Her young friend agrees that one cannot live the life of these heroes: "No one would marry if this were possible only after eighty years of martyrdom" (OD, 91). The ideas expressed are those of *Pharsamon*. Indeed, says the coquette, "if fickleness were punished by death, men and women would be falling by platoons" (OD, 76).

This attitude does not deny the need for sentiment. On the contrary. The coquette wants to see her lover passionate. She lent him the *Lettres de la Religieuse Portugaise (Letters of the Portuguese Nun* by Guilleragues, a story of desperate love), and the return of the book becomes the setting of their next encounter (OD, 98). Lending him such a book was a trick, an artifice; Marivaux always implies that artifice is germane to love, that nothing can guarantee eternal happiness, especially not the happy ending of a comedy! To him, heroic passions are not of this world and love must be artfully maintained.

This attitude, which we can term a "realistic" one, caused Voltaire's malicious comment that Marivaux did not know passion but only "spider webs," the byways rather than the grand road of love, but it is also true that Voltaire's description of grand passion, in his comedies and tragedies, is utterly old-fashioned and dead, while Marivaux' new realism is still very much alive. The dialogue of the two girls combines elements of pathos with the understanding of man's desires and flightiness, in the spirit of Marivaux' theater which was now to become his principal occupation.

XI L'Amour et la Vérité
(Love and Truth),
comedy in three acts in collaboration with Saint-Jory, T. I., 1720, extant as a fragment.

Of Marivaux' first contribution to the repertoire of the Italian troupe, there remains only a dialogue which appeared in the *Mercure* soon after the first and only performance. Love converses with Truth and complains that Cupid (sensuality) perverts today's lovers and makes Plutus (money) more appealing than Venus (beauty). "Sometimes you don't need love to be happy!" Truth replies: "Most lovers owe their success to moments like those" (T I, 64). In this context, "to be happy" can only refer to sexual gratification. Marivaux' theme is that of several of his novels and stories of the past: idealistic everlasting love is not of this world. It is most important to note that the framework of allegory, the setting in an imaginary landscape, do not preclude a hearty realism.

Love is suitably pessimistic: "Man's heart isn't worth much" (T I, 65), neither are marriage contracts: "People forced to love each other don't suit me. It's wrong to expect a rogue like myself to stick to the intent of a contract" (T I, 67). Love feels so out of touch with the world that he will hide in a tree and wait for a shepherd to meet his shepherdess under its branches; he will then be able to influence them surreptitiously. Truth finds an even more paradoxical solution. In accord with the proverb that says: "Truth is at the bottom of a well," i.e., truth is deep, she will take refuge in a well and poison the waters of the spring, so that the unsuspecting will drink a kind of serum of truth (T I, 68). Love and Truth hiding and masked while the world goes on its merry way is a theme characteristic of Marivaux.

The Italian players who were performing this play were just beginning to use French dialogue and had a great deal of difficulty mastering the language. The troupe, directed by Luigi Riccoboni, had been invited after Louis XIV had died (the king had expelled an earlier Italian troupe in 1697) and settled at the Hôtel de Bourgogne in 1716. The interruption of almost twenty years meant that the public of Paris was no longer used to Italian, nor to seeing improvised plays, for the tradition of the *commedia dell'arte* provided nothing more than plot outlines and let each actor play his customary part by making up not only lines, but jokes and funny motions *(lazzi).* To break the impasse, Riccoboni wrote a play with a more normal structure, an adaptation of a plot of Dancourt, entitled *Generous in Spite of Himself* (1717), in which a miser is forced to marry his daughters to their respective lovers, but language was far more of a barrier than the type of play. Therefore Riccoboni contracted scripts in French with Piron, Boissy, and especially Marivaux, also Autreau, Fuzelier, and Delisle de la Drévetière, whose work was to furnish him elements of his plots. The first play produced largely in French was Autreau's *Naufrage du Port-à-l'Anglais (Shipwreck at Port England)*, 1718, in which Lelio, on a business trip on the Seine, marries off two daughters. Between 1720 and 1740, Marivaux was to furnish twenty comedies to the troupe, while submitting only eight to the French Theater (Comédie Française).

The principal actors were the following: Luigi Riccoboni, called Lelio on the state; he played the father, or Pantalon, who usually represents a doctor, a sensuous and ridiculous old man, or the part of a refined lover; Lelio's roles were most often adapted to his moody, pessimistic personality. After 1725, these roles were gradually transferred to Jean Romagnesi; Riccoboni retired with his wife in 1729 to devote himself to historical and religious writing. His wife, Elena Balletti, Flaminia on the stage, played feminine leads until they were passed on to Silvia around 1723; Flaminia also performed as the second lady or the maid.

Mario Balletti, her brother and Silvia's husband, acted in supporting roles, while Silvia (her actual name, Zanetta Benozzi) became Marivaux' outstanding interpreter. She was the greatest actress of her time and played his roles with success as late as the 1750's. A touching tribute to her is contained in Casanova's *Mémoires* (ed. Pléiade, I, 634-35).

Thomassin Vicentini was Arlequin, an actor with superb skill. He knew how to rouse the audience to hilarious laughter, also to tears. His death in 1739 left everyone disconsolate. Another invaluable member of the troupe was Dominique Biancolelli as Trivelin, the clever servant. He was the only member of the old Italian troupe to join the new; his experience in Paris and his knowledge of French were important. He died in 1734.

Marivaux knew how to put these actors to best use. He created parts with their individual qualities in mind. The pair, Lelio and Arlequin, enabled him to include master and servant in mutually supporting roles not unlike Don Quixote and Sancho Panza. He kept in mind their skill for pantomime, he even made special use of the fact Arlequin habitually wore a black face mask. By providing them parts well suited to their skills, he greatly facilitated their task of performing in French and enabled them to portray subtle emotions in spite of their accent. Thus Marivaux created his means of success.

CHAPTER 4

Success on the Stage

I Arlequin Poli par l'Amour
(Harlequin Polished by Love),
comedy in one act, T.I., 1720.

MARIVAUX' first comedy independently written for the Italian players is justly famous. The stage directions that happen to be unusually complete show how carefully he planned for pantomime and used the actor's skills. The meeting of Silvia and Arlequin is notable. Arlequin enters playing with a shuttlecock, like a child. It falls down, and as he picks it up, he perceives Silvia; he is so struck by her beauty that he can only gradually recover his upright position. Their naïve manners are hilarious. Greedily Arlequin kisses her fingers: "I never tasted goodies that good" *(de bonbon si bon),* T I, 94.

Their love threatens the plans of the Fairy Queen who wanted Arlequin for herself. She justifies her desire for the attractive boy who is much younger than she, by saying: "Nothing is so natural as loving what is loveable" (T I, 87), but she is unwilling to let the maxim apply to others. Her desire for Arlequin seems grotesque, her use of power seems unjust and barbarous. It is a characteristic paradox that in this fairy world only the Fairy Queen is unattractive.

Trivelin, the Queen's prime minister, defects from her cause; he tells Arlequin how to cope with her: "Swear that you love her, then cleverly and playfully try to get hold of her wand!" (T I, 106) The trick works and the Fairy Queen becomes his prisoner. She is furious. Arlequin admonishes: "Quiet now, I am the master, look sweetly at me!" Silvia, in what may seem like a pun on the "usefulness" and appeal of virtue, suggests they release her: "Let us be generous; compassion is a great quality!" (T I, 109), and so Arlequin sets her free but keeps Silvia. Love has indeed "polished him," i.e., made him not only polite *(poli)* but knowing in the ways of the world, and powerful!

A number of sources for the play have been identified, plays by Autreau and Fuzelier, a short story by Mme Durand-Bédacier, entitled

The Miracle of Love; a parallel in *Persiles and Sigismunda* by Cervantes has been mentioned. They show that Marivaux, much like Shakespeare, is not an inventor of plots and that his originality lies in his form, style, and the magic of his characterizations. One comparison is particularly interesting, the parallel between *Arlequin Poli* and Racine's *Phèdre.* Phèdre loves Hyppolite just as the Fairy Queen loves Arlequin; in each case the young man foils the Queen; Hyppolite loves Aricie and goes to his death before Phèdre can claim him. Of course Marivaux wrote no tragedy, but the touching quality of young love is common to both plays and Arlequin stands closer to Hyppolite than to Agnès in Molière's *Ecole des Femmes (School for Women),* though Agnès, like Arlequin, finds ways to outwit age and experience. Marivaux' admiration for Classical tragedy is ever present and the example bears out the theoretical statements of 1719.

II   Annibal (Hannibal),
tragedy in 5 acts in verse. T.F., 1720.

Marivaux hoped to establish himself on the French stage as well, but somehow the Comédie Française never brought him satisfaction. His one and only complete tragedy was particularly poorly received. It convinced him that he could do better in the natural prose style of comedy.[1]

Annibal is an antiheroic tragedy with an heroic ending! The hero is pictured in his old age, a defeated warrior who has found refuge at the court of Prusias and has been promised his daughter, Laodice, in marriage; only it so happens that the Roman ambassador, Flaminius, has loved her in times past and now returns to claim her for himself. Besides, Flaminius wants to break up the alliance which seems dangerous for Rome. A remarkable passage describes how Laodice first met Flaminius. As she recalls the birth of love, we are reminded of Arlequin setting eyes on Silvia: "My eyes were proud. They met his and his easily conquered mine. I was moved from the depth of my heart. I could neither escape nor sustain his look" (T I, 124).

Under such circumstances, it is clear that Laodice will prefer Flaminius, but she feels sympathy for Annibal; she wants to protect him from her father, Prusias, a weak and cowardly king, who has withdrawn his support from Annibal in favor of the more powerful Romans. For this reason, Laodice sets a condition to her marriage to Flaminius. She will become his wife if he will protect Annibal, i.e., violate his instructions from Rome and his professional ethics. "Would

you accept a suitor who preferred you to faith and honor?" Flaminius
asks Laodice. She replies: "Why not give up your exalted idea of
honor?" (T I, 160). A heroine in a traditional tragedy would have given
the opposite response. The spirit of compromise fits Marivaux' attitude
as a "Modern," but is ill-suited to this tragedy which suddenly shifts to
the heroic mold in which the author must have felt most
uncomfortable.

Prusias has treacherously urged Annibal to flee and let the Romans
capture him. Thus compromise becomes impossible. Annibal rises to his
former glory and poisons himself, exclaiming: "I die but lose only my
life!" (T I, 172). Laodice is theoretically free to marry Flaminius now
the obstacle has been removed, but, like the Princesse de Clèves (in the
novel of Mme de Lafayette), she rejects her lover with violence. After
all, he has broken her trust and left Annibal no choice but suicide or an
ignominious death in Rome.

Thus, after four acts of a new kind of tragedy, with suggestions of
ambiguous compromises, a fifth, heroic act provides solutions clearly at
odds with Marivaux' philosophy. One confirmation: only two years
after he portrayed Annibal's suicide, he criticizes Montesquieu for
defending the right to take one's life (OD, 154 of 1722). Besides,
Marivaux must have felt out of his element drawing on Livy and
Plutarch and on *Nicomède* by Corneille in order to evoke antiquity like
the "Ancients" he made fun of.

III   Le Spectateur Français
(The French Spectator),
periodical in 25 issues (feuilles),
1721-24, issued as a volume in 1728.

The *Spectator* of Addison and Steele had been an outstanding
success; imitations were numerous and known to Marivaux, especially
those of Van Effen; translations of the *Spectator* had begun to appear
in 1714, but the perplexing fact is that Marivaux at times imitated
passages that had not as yet appeared in French; they must have been
discussed in salons for, in spite of the monumental thesis of Lucette
Desvignes-Parent, it is not proven he knew English. The pattern of
Addison and Steele fitted him perfectly. He adopted a tone, purposely
whimsical, a method of random comments in great variety without
imitating particulars too closely.

Thus he set out to "capture the thoughts chance inspires" (OD,
114-17), frivolous, fortuitous, but also pertinent, forceful, and concise

(OD, 114-16, 139), an "orgy of ideas" *(libertinage d'idées,* OD, 132), gathered at random. To amuse the reader, he changes topic frequently and excuses his apparent lack of plan and method by claiming they are the result of laziness (OD, 117, 252). The term must not mislead us, for beside the twenty-five issues of the *Spectateur,* Marivaux composed three comedies during the same period. His *Lettre sur la Paresse, 1740 (Letter on Laziness,* OD, 443-44), credits laziness with enabling him to write without interruptions and other concerns. Laziness refers to the reluctance to formulate ideas unless carefully conceived or to continue writing when he has said enough.

To stake out his claim to wisdom, Marivaux assumes the age of Madame de Lambert; he poses as an old man of seventy-four (OD 207). Madame de Lambert's conversations, and also her published work, inspired many passages; for instance, the theory of man's natural infidelity (OD, 203) is found in her *Treatise on Friendship,*[2] and her books giving *Advice to a Son* and *to a Daughter* provided other ideas like the suffering that naturally accompanies love.

An important theme, here as elsewhere, is sentiment. We cannot resist passions; indeed, the passions furnish us insights inaccessible to reason, i.e., to traditional, systematic philosophy (OD, 227, 232). Marivaux admits that he likes to savor his emotions in order not to "lose a single part of grief and compassion for those who suffer" (OD, 129). It is their emotional impact that makes him sing the praises of *Romulus* and *Inez de Castro,* two tragedies by his friend, La Motte, that today leave us cold (OD, 123, 227).

Love is no dream of peaceful happiness. Two girls complain that they were undone because they believed their lovers to be gentlemen (OD, 155, 165). A wife who wants to remain faithful to her husband appeals to the honor of her lover and miraculously gets him to leave and thus preserves her innocence, but she admits how much his attentions had flattered her; "an ugly woman would have been respected with less trouble" (OD, 212, cf. 122-23). The virtuous wife whose very virtue makes her so attractive, better be on her guard (OD, 162). Like Saint-Evremont, Marivaux is an Epicurean who regards virtue as infinitely attractive (OD, 162-63, 217, 260) and speaks of the "voluptuous satisfaction" of doing good (OD, 132).

Since innocence and virtue are in constant danger, none of this expresses an easy optimism. A good example is the story of his return to the home of a girl with whom he was much taken, because he had forgotten a glove. He finds her sitting in front of a mirror, practicing the wiles that entranced him. This shock, he tells us, makes him break with her for good: "Now I know the machines of the opera, it interests me less" (OD, 118). And thus, he pretends that he became an unalterable misanthrope.

This account is no more autobiographical than its companion piece which provides a contrary view. He tells us that a woman without makeup and artifice is not truly herself. Love requires means to entice (*piquer,* OD 201). Besides, Marivaux is no misanthrope. He is not at all like Hermocrate, whom he pictures ready to withdraw to a desert as a hermit because he has found that kindness leaves him powerless and little respected (OD, 179-86). Marivaux is no Alceste; he remains in the world, he is a realist; he is not shocked by artifice and ambiguity; he describes marriage as fraught with constant dangers. The marriage partners must continuously find ways to reawaken love (OD, 201-2), for being accustomed to one another is insufficient for happiness. He also reports the dream of a Spaniard, a kind of "topography" of love with a warning that there is a "monster" inside Love's palace (OD, 142).

Marivaux strikes a balance. He calls virtue infinitely attractive, but feels that this very appeal breeds danger. The generous Hermocrate makes everyone jealous (OD, 180-85) while flatterers succeed (OD, 199, 252). The tone of these descriptions is humorous, but there are moments when Marivaux turns into an intransigent and pessimistic idealist. The evil, he tells us, are shamed by the righteous (OD, 260); the rewards of vice are too brutish to be satisfying (OD, 206, 260); atheists (*esprits forts* as in La Bruyère) "brazenly walk in darkness" and are themselves the best argument for religion (OD, 197). In essays of 1751 and 1754, he speaks of the impotence of the honest man *(honnête homme),* the most valuable subject of his prince, the one to be trusted before all others. Such statements break with the dominant humor and lighthearted acceptance of man's ambiguity, but Marivaux does not remain entrenched for long in his extreme position. The strong attack on atheists, for instance, is matched by a comment that many sermons express the priest's vanity (OD, 195) and that ever so many pious ladies are really in love with their confessors (OD, 224).

Still, some moments of extreme bitterness stand out. They concern the abuses of wealth. Having lost his modest fortune, Marivaux speaks from experience. The wealthy fear those who seek their aid; they humiliate them (OD, 116). Wealth corrupts. An unfeeling son neglects his father after inheriting all his money (OD, 186-88, cf. *Marianne,* Pt. XI). Gaudy clothing is a hateful show of wealth; to escape such a display when the Spanish Infanta arrived in Paris (March, 1722),

Marivaux takes refuge in a barrelmaker's shop (OD, 133). He speaks of
a girl who would have been ruined by the offensive propositions of a
wealthy libertine, had he not given her all the money he carried on him
and enabled her to resist (OD, 129).

Around 1723-24 there are further attacks on the abuses of wealth,
on the humiliation of the poor (OD 256-67). In one disillusioned scene,
autobiography is barely camouflaged. A woman (actually Marivaux
himself) comes to see a lady; as she steps up to embrace her, she finds
that this friend just died of a heart attack (OD, 222). Marivaux' wife
must have died this way. The story speaks of a son, ten years old, while
Marivaux' daughter was only four, but the parallel is evident and gives
special meaning to the plea to seize the happiness of every moment, for
it may have eternal consequences (OD, 208). This statement made
Georges Poulet present Marivaux as a precursor of Existentialism
(Etudes sur le Temps Humain), but this may be an inopportune
extension of Marivaux' pessimism. The fact remains that he was greatly
affected by his limited social condition and by the loss of his wife. This
was the time when he composed several comedies without happy
endings, like *La Fausse Suivante.*

Basically, Marivaux attempts to remain impersonal and humorous.
He inserts a burlesque letter from a husband whose wife is a miser. To
get even with her, he has embarked on ruinous expenses and hopes the
shock of finding this out will kill her; yet he regrets his course; she is
too pretty to die! (OD, 172-76) Most of the time, Marivaux dissociates
himself from categorical positions in defense of virtue or opposition to
vice, for he is resolutely "Modern," and associates moralizing literature
with an outmoded past. In this connection he returns several times to
his party position opposing the "Ancients." The worshipers of antiquity
deny the merit of contemporary literature; to make fun of them, he
tells us that he found groceries wrapped in a sheet of the *Iliad;* Homer
must be turning in his grave! (OD, 146-49, 159). He laughs at those
who judge a work by its number of pages; the thicker it is, the more
philosophical it is supposed to be (OD, 137-39). He affirms that he is
writing for his own times and therefore must not emulate the past (OD,
148). He is proud of the wit and intelligence *(esprit)* of his own day;
without pursuing it for its own sake, he wants to remain natural and
express himself in terms characteristically his own *(rester dans la
singularité d'esprit qui nous est échue,* OD, 144-49).

This remarkable formulation of his literary objective seemed so
absurd to his critic, the abbé Desfontaines, that he quoted it to make
fun of Marivaux and did not even feel the need to explain why it was

inadequate (in the *Dictionnaire Néologique*). Marivaux felt that Desfontaines' comments were too personal and, therefore, offensive (OD, 137, 246). He became so angry that he suspended the *Spectateur* for four months (OD, 143). Then he counterattacked: critics, he says, are like women unable to bear the beauty of a rival (OD, 150-55); they rarely recognize talent (OD, 134) while he would give credit where credit is due, e.g., to Montesquieu and his *Lettres Persanes (Persian Letters*, OD, 153-54).

Once again we find a rather stark expression of personal feelings. Marivaux aims at a witty tone but often cannot hide his position. He wants to "penetrate the minds of men" (OD, 127), but he also establishes a doctrine, and shows a passionate humanism that is barely concealed. The difficulty is to define a code of conduct, toward critics, toward other authors, and his neighbors in general, when he knows that didactic tracts will be discarded by the modern reader. He must sweeten the pill:

Let us be good and virtuous . . . . What I can reasonably want another to do for me, even though he may fail to act that way, shows me what I must do for him . . . . We may be born evil, but we bear our evil like a monster we must fight . . . . As soon as we become members of society, we are forced to observe an order that shields us from our evil impulses. Reason which reveals this need to us, is itself the corrective of our iniquity. (OD, 233-34)

This attitude implies a kind of psychology. "We are the object, or rather the subject of this science we should like to possess" (OD, 232). Just as in 1749-50, before the French Academy, he proposes a "science of the human heart," in the *Spectateur,* he attempts to formulate it as amusingly as possible; he presents serious considerations not as his own, but as those submitted by an unknown reader (OD, 231-32). In the *Spectateur* and other journals to follow, he sets forth many of the principles which his plays and novels illustrate.

IV   La Surprise de l'Amour
(The Surprise of Love),
comedy in 3 acts, T.I., 1722.

The three comedies produced while he edited the *Spectateur,* rank among Marivaux' best. These are important years in his career, during which he turned into a major dramatist. Meanwhile Silvia played an ever more important role in the Italian troupe, second only to that of Lelio in *La Surprise;* she played the lead in *La Fausse Suivante.* Lesbros de la Versane tells an anecdote that took place during the rehearsals of *La Surprise.* One day Marivaux came to watch, incognito; he volunteered to read part of her role. "You read so well, you are the author of the devil!" she exclaimed. He indicated that he was not the devil *(L'Esprit de Marivaux,* p. 16). Nothing is known to confirm or deny that this meeting took place; we are not informed about their actual relations. Paul Gazagne (in *Marivaux par lui-même)* indulges in pure fantasy when he sees them as lovers; he also goes too far when he asserts that, in Marivaux' plays, marriage is an euphemism for surrender, and love for sensual desire.

La Surprise de l'Amour inverts the plot of the early novels. It begins with two disappointed lovers who foreswear love like Alceste at the end of the *Misanthrope.* They will withdraw from the world like Hermocrate in the *Spectateur.* Obviously they have drawn the wrong conclusion from past experience but they will be the last to know it. As a dutiful servant, Arlequin attempts to adopt his master's pessimism. The spectator will smile as Arlequin finds temptation all around him. He wants to step across the way in order not to see two birds in a tree. "I swore to forego love but when I see it, I almost feel like violating my resolve" (T I, 190). Lelio tells him women are vipers. "But they are such pretty animals," replies Arlequin, "such lovely kittens. What a shame they have so many claws" (T I, 192). Here he is upholding Lelio's position to Colombine, the maid of the Countess:

COLOMBINE: Why are you and your master such misanthropes?
ARLEQUIN: Because the proverb says, a scalded cat fears the water.
COLOMBINE: Explain! Why is Lelio avoiding my mistress?
ARLEQUIN: Because we know love and what it is worth. (T I, 197)

Unencumbered by the rules of etiquette and conceptions of honor, less subject to resentments, the servants will recognize their desire to marry long before their masters but stage conventions require that they wait until their masters are ready for the ceremony. This makes them like their masters' alter egos. Once they understand the situation, the servants can do much to hasten the conclusion.

In this manner, Colombine helps Arlequin to see the light:

COLOMBINE: This fellow is fighting his own desires as if he were a gentleman.
ARLEQUIN: Aren't you ashamed of being so pretty? (T I, 206)

Very soon Arlequin gives up the battle against love, but Lelio takes to the end of the play to come to the same conclusion: "Today I have no taste for the role of a gentleman. I am tired of that little matter" (T I, 231). Just how much self-deception he had to overcome is clear when he tells the Countess before the final conversion: "If I loved you, I would be the most humiliated, the most ridiculed and pitiful of all men who might conceivably love you" (T I, 220). He even imagined that he was carrying the Countess' portrait on his person only because it resembled a friend of his (T I, 230).

Love is presented on three levels: (1) Jacqueline, a maid, and Pierre, the gardener, are ready to marry from the start. Arrangements for them become a pretext for meetings between Lelio and the Countess. Pierre philosophizes: "No harm in loving one's neighbor, especially if she is pretty" (T I, 188), and Jacqueline likes his advances. They are so much children of nature that there is only one danger: Pierre might fall for Thomas' daughter if there is much of a delay. (2) Arlequin and Colombine, beset by their masters' hesitations, struggle until the second act. (3) Lelio and the Countess battle until the end of the third.

When Colombine tells Lelio that all of his actions betray love, he replies: "But how was I to know?" Arlequin adds: "It isn't my fault, I warned you!" (T I, 232). Finally, Lelio must choose between the yoke *(tyrannie)* of marriage and the insult *(grossièreté)* of saying "no" (T I, 231). "You are the master," says the Countess.–"Of what?"–"To love or not to love" (T I, 235). He says "yes" and Arlequin can marry Colombine "without ceremony," i.e., without further ado, but there is a pun: Repeatedly Marivaux expresses the idea that the ceremony adds nothing if there is love. Love had already stated this in *L'Amour et la Vérité;* but had it not taken three acts of "ceremony" in *La Surprise* to come to this conclusion?

Of the fairy world in *Arlequin Poli,* there remains only the circle the Baron draws around Lelio and the Countess to tie them together as by enchantment. The atmosphere has become mundane, with practical matters like Pierre's marriage serving to draw the two misanthropes into each other's trap. It is characteristic of Marivaux to find two such persons who are forced to give up their foolish principles, for principles or gems of wisdom, like proverbs, grandly enunciated are generally misconceived or misunderstood. Marivaux' "maxims," like those of La Rochefoucauld, merely emphasize the ambiguity of truth and man's illusions.

To compose his play, Marivaux turned to the repertoire of the first and second Italian troupes, including plays by Riccoboni and Autreau (and thus, indirectly to Moreto); while disillusioned lovers are common also in Molière, his situations are different. Marivaux avoids following him as a model!

V La Double Inconstance
(Two Cases of Infidelity),
comedy in 3 acts, T.I., 1723.

Marivaux' preferred play retells, in comic form for the stage, the tale of the rape of Bastille, in *La Voiture Embourbée* (R, 47-68), and there are parallels to another melodramatic episode in the *Spectateur,* the story of Eléonore who mortified Mirski by substituting her maid for herself because she foresaw that Mirski would abandon her (OD, 163-72). Marivaux must have been particularly proud of the way he was able to camouflage the tragic theme of seduction. The technique is inspired by the conventions of Classical tragedy which, e.g., proscribes death from the stage but does not hide the fact violence occurs. Thus the inherent cruelty of the story remains even in the fairy kingdom of *La Double Inconstance* where a charming Prince is committed, by the law of the land, to marry one of his subjects without doing violence to her feelings.

When the play begins, Arlequin and Silvia love each other; when it ends, they both marry another partner. Their estrangement is gradual, the alienation of affection almost imperceptible, and yet it is carefully planned by the Prince who uses a disguise and a number of assistants to succeed. The rape of Bastille lurks in the background. Jean Anouilh, perhaps unaware of the parallel, sensed the tragic theme when he interpreted the action, in his play, *La Répétition (The Rehearsal),* as a plan for seduction.

This does not inhibit comedy. Arlequin is funny when he protests against the abuse of wealth and power. From the start he distrusts the "honor" of having the Prince provide him with a servant, i.e., of seeing the spy, Trivelin, assigned to follow him about (T I, 262). Later on the Prince offers patents of nobility in exchange for Silvia. Arlequin wonders whether an edict can make him into a gentleman *(honnête homme)*; it seems that often such patents dispense their holders from honorable conduct *(honnêteté)*, for the "honor" of noblemen seems frequently as dubious as their motives (T I, 305). "The Prince," says Arlequin, "is a gentleman. If he had not stolen my mistress, I might like him a lot" (T I, 280). Eventually Arlequin succumbs. He has rejected the advances of Lisette (sent by the Prince) who was all too forward, but when Flaminia comes to sympathize, serves good food and excellent wine and displays charm and kindness, he falls in love with her; Flaminia effectively supports the plans of the Prince without Arlequin noticing it.

Silvia's fate is similar, and here too the action provides a great deal of humor. At the outset, she rejects the very idea of being courted by the Prince: "A decent girl must love her husband, and I could never love you" (T I, 256). At that, she does not know to whom she is talking to, for the Prince is disguised as one of his own officers. "Better a commoner content in her little village than a princess weeping in a luxurious apartment" (T I, 257). At the end of the play she will be only too happy to marry the Prince and she won't be weeping in his luxurious apartment! The Prince is very clever. He will not reveal his identity until he is sure of Silvia's love. She would never have yielded to the advantages of rank, she had too noble a soul for that. Indeed, it is her sensitive, noble soul that makes her discover a special kinship in the Prince and repells her from Arlequin who seems vulgar when he leaves her to taste Flaminia's good food and wine. Silvia seems born to be noble and to marry the Prince; her very delicacy makes the seduction succeed so easily. Meanwhile, Lisette, Flaminia, Trivelin, all paid assistants of the Prince, have unobtrusively advanced his cause; disguise, along with rapid, witty dialogue have done much to camouflage the plans that propel the action.

A reviewer in the *Mercure* finds there is too much analysis of delicate feelings; he objects to Marivaux' "metaphysics of the heart" (T I, 247), a reproach used by Voltaire and others, who disliked psychological comedy. They overlooked that there is considerable social comment in Marivaux' play. The setting in a fairy kingdom has not infringed on the understanding, and portrayal of political and social reality.

VI   Le Prince Travesti
(The Prince in Disguise),
comedy in 3 acts, T.I., 1724.

The underlying pessimism of the years 1723-24, which we discovered in the *Spectateur* and in *La Double Inconstance,* becomes even more manifest in the following plays. In *Le Prince Travesti* we find, for the first time, a character who is fundamentally evil, Frédéric, the despicable counselor of the Princess, always ready for a deal and for a bribe. To him we can apply the following comment from the *Spectateur:*

An evil man is always evil . . . . only, when he is surrounded by honors and has high rank with important functions . . . things look different . . . , evil is masked . . . , even its excesses are embellished . . . . That is why . . . in high stations disrepute usually brings honor, whereas ordinary people like ourselves are reduced to shame for the slightest fault. (OD, 242-43)

In *La Double Inconstance,* deceit was justified in the name of love; in the next two plays it makes an even bolder appearance though the comic tone is preserved.

The Classical triangle, Lelio, The Princess, Hortense, corresponds to a large extent to Racine's Bajazet, Roxane, Atalide, and Frédéric can be compared with Acomat. The Princess who becomes the rival in love of her own confidente, Hortense, also appears in Corneille's *Cid,* but, more to the point, there is a parallel situation in *Les Effets Surprenants* where Frédélingue, before he can marry Parménie, finds himself pursued by a princess who resents Parménie as her rival. Frédélingue has won the love of Parménie by an heroic rescue just as Lelio has rescued Hortense. Enough is said to show that the noble deeds of tragedy and romance are very much present in Marivaux' comedy. He has, in fact, created a new genre which combines sentiment with heroic comedy of the type of Molière's *Dom Garcie de Navarre. Le Prince Travesti* goes further in this direction than other plays of Marivaux. It is not surprising to find that he also produced a version in 5 acts (T I, 330).

The Princess of Barcelona is negotiating her marriage to the King of Castille. She does not know that the ambassador she is talking to is the King himself in disguise. She would proceed immediately, had she not fallen in love with Lelio whom she has appointed to be her prime minister, much to the displeasure of Frédéric who wants the post for himself. Now Frédéric needs Lelio to support his cause. He offers him his daughter as a reward. When he is refused on both counts, he becomes furious. Lelio, actually the King of Leon, also in disguise, does not reciprocate the feelings of the Princess because he fell in love with her confidante, Hortense, when he rescued her some time ago from highway robbers. Both recall the event as the most significant of their lives. It occurred before the death of the husband of Hortense. Hers has been an unhappy marriage which left her as disillusioned as the Countess in *La Surprise.*

Frédéric schemes to defeat the power of Lelio, but he accomplishes little. He attempts to bribe Lelio's valet, Arlequin, but is powerless in the face of Arlequin's lack of discretion, which is one of the main resources of comedy in the play. Frédéric offers him money, a ring, even a pretty girl, if he will spy on his master. Arlequin is impressed with the gifts and ready to accept them, but he will tell all to Lelio and the Princess:

FRÉDÉRIC: You miserable fellow, you are bent on dishonoring me.
ARLEQUIN: Eh! When one isn't honorable, why does one need the reputation of having honor?
FRÉDÉRIC: If you tell them, you scoundrel, my vengeance will be terrifying . . . . But someone might approach . . ., let's get on with it. I shall pay the price you ask for your silence. How much do you want?
ARLEQUIN: Watch it! It won't be cheap!
FREDERIC: Let's hear what you want. Your finagling is killing me!
ARLEQUIN: Look, the idea of being a gentleman appeals to me . . . . Why don't you present your request in a more formal style and call me "Sir" for a while? Let me be Frédéric and you be Arlequin. (T I, 356-57)

The scene is hilarious. It resembles Scene 4 of a parody of Voltaire's *Artémire,* composed by the Italian troupe, which shows that Marivaux adopted dialogue from many sources. In any event, Arlequin accepts the money and the ring, but tells all. Unwittingly he helps Frédéric, for Hortense has also confided in him and asked him to deliver her love letter to Lelio. Arlequin delivers it to the Princess who becomes so upset and jealous that she jails Lelio. It looks as if Frédéric might yet win out.

But now the King of Castille enters heroically into action. He may be Lelio's rival, or so he thinks, for the love of the Princess, but he will not let the honorable Lelio be defeated by a vile creature like Frédéric; indeed, he tells Lelio, when he later finds out that he is the King of Leon: "Your rank does not surprise me; it corresponds to the sentiments you have shown!" (T I, 394). The King of Castille pleads for Lelio with the Princess, and she, in turn, is eventually reconciled with Hortense, and this is a touching scene. Frédéric, on the other hand, is put in his place by Hortense: "We will have to kill you to deliver you from the sad fate of being hateful to everyone; that is the best we can do for you!" (T I, 381). And later: "I am no longer seeking your aid. You are too wicked to be feared. Your evil spirit is so manifest that you cannot hurt anyone but yourself!" (T I, 392). Is this comedy? The tone varies; humor alternates with heroic action, fury, tenderness, moral apostrophe, much as in a novel or in the *Spectateur*. The Princess will marry the King of Castille because his intervention on Lelio's behalf was so noble; virtue, as we read in the *Spectateur,* is infinitely attractive.

So love is born, and this leaves Lelio free to marry Hortense. The disguise of the two kings enables them to observe the person they hope to marry; as in the *Jeu de L'Amour,* the mask provides perspective. Virtue wins out just as it will in Marivaux' major novels, perhaps because he knew reality to be different. It is a characteristic paradox. Broad laughter is provided primarily by Arlequin. Thus comedy has come to include a great number of moods, some quite tragic and bitter, and some tender, like the victory of friendship in the reconciliation of the Princess with Hortense. *Le Prince Travesti* is a complex play and an interesting one.

VII   La Fausse Suivante
(The False Servant),
comedy in 3 acts, T.I., 1724.

This time it is Silvia who wears the disguise. Her marriage to Lelio is being discussed; she wants to observe her intended husband. Dressed as the Chevalier (a small nobleman), she becomes Lelio's valet and finds him interested only in her money. He had first planned to marry a Countess with the annual income of six thousand francs; now he has set his mind on Silvia who is twice as rich! He knows her only as a girl from Paris whom he has not met. There is one complication. If he breaks with the Countess, he owes her thirty thousand francs, but not if she breaks with him. For this reason Lelio asks the Chevalier to court the Countess. He wants her to fall in love with him (her):

CHEVALIER: I don't have much inclination for this kind of marriage.
LELIO: Why not?
CHEVALIER: For ever so many reasons. For one, I could never love the Countess.
LELIO: Who is asking you to love her? Must one love one's wife? If you don't love her, that's just too bad for her; that's her business, not yours.
CHEVALIER: Oh, I thought one had to love one's wife, for if one doesn't, one lives on bad terms with her.
LELIO: Well, so much the better. If you are on bad terms with her, you don't have to see her, and that's all to the good.

CHEVALIER: You win! I am ready to do as you wish and marry the Countess. I can always count on my good friend, Lelio, to strengthen my conviction that one owes one's wife nothing but disdain.

LELIO: There I shall set you an excellent example! You don't by any chance think that I'm going to love that girl from Paris? A couple of weeks, at most; after that I shall be completely tired of her . . .

CHEVALIER: Did they tell you that she is pretty?

LELIO: The letter says that she is, but the way I feel, that won't do her much good. If she is not ugly now, she will surely become ugly being my wife. It can't fail? (T I, 424-25)

Under such circumstances, all Silvia can think of is to ruin his vile schemes. She makes sure that he must pay the thirty thousand francs and lose both chances to marry. That is no happy ending! The undertone is one of bitterness, and of resolve to avenge the victims of such scoundrels as Lelio, or Frédéric in the preceding play. The *Spectateur* expresses Marivaux' disillusionment of this period in these terms:

If I stated earlier that my stories could be of some profit to my readers, I no longer lay claim to such grand results, for I know men read only to be amused, and the pleasure of amusing them no longer tempts me. (OD, 253)

This is a half-truth, for the *Spectateur* as well as *La Fausse Suivante* do amuse, but the sadness of 1723-24 is barely hidden.

The play was written for Silvia; she was a great success in the role of the Chevalier. Her greatest scene is when she wins the love of the Countess. Another hilarious moment is Trivelin's discovery, from Frontin, that the Chevalier is a girl in disguise; so Trivelin tells her: "I shall be your valet on the stage and your lover behind the scenery" (T I, 420). Trivelin has an interesting part in the first act. He appears as a true *pícaro* with his meager bundle of possessions, and tells of his stormy career, "sometimes master, sometimes servant" (T I, 412). His explanations to Frontin of two gangs, the "Ancients" whose captain is Homer, and the "Moderns who do not go back four thousand years," are very funny (T I, 414) and represent a humorous restatement of Marivaux' position. However, the role of Trivelin becomes insignificant later on and he is no Figaro. The revolutionary, if there is one in this play (cf. Arlequin in *La Double Inconstance*), is the Chevalier: Silvia fights injustice, i.e., Lelio's plan; she defends women's rights, her own!

Gustave Lanson has shown how frequently the girl disguised as a man, following her lover, occurs in literature,[3] but the most interesting parallel occurs in Shakespeare. In *Twelfth Night,* Viola becomes the valet of the man she loves just like Silvia, and like her is asked to court a Countess (Olivia) who then falls in love with her. The difference in tone is great, for the Chevalier stages a seduction scene while Viola goes to Olivia much against her will; her devotion to Duke Orsino is infinite. Shakespeare portrays the victory of sweet love, Marivaux, vengeance against a Don Juan. Besides, Shakespeare's range of emotions is far greater, from the outrageous jokes directed against Malvoglio and rough humor unthinkable in eighteenth-century France, to lyrical love. It is not a case of influence, but of a common source, Bandello, that explains the parallel. The story of Bandello reached Marivaux through the repertoire of the Italian troupe and Shakespeare through the Belleforest translation. It provides an instructive comparison, for *La Fausse Suivante* shows Marivaux at his best.

VIII Le Dénouement Imprévu
(The Unforeseen Solution),
comedy in one act, T. F., 1724.

Finally Marivaux succeeds in having a comedy accepted by the Comédie Française. It was a fair success, but soon the play disappeared from the repertoire. Marivaux did not come into his own on this stage until well after his death; still, he never ceased submitting plays. *Le Dénouement Imprévu* is brief, excellent, and, according to Lessing, Marivaux' best work.

The title is a typical paradox. Mademoiselle Argante marries the suitor chosen by her father, but only after making determined efforts to foil his plan, and pretending to be mad, not like Lucinde in *Le Médecin Malgré Lui* (Molière's *Doctor in Spite of Himself*) who claimed to have lost her speech, but most articulately so. Later, her haste to marry the man chosen for her and the precipitous ending are hilarious.

Eraste, the young man whom her father has invited, arrives much like Dorante in the *Jeu de l'Amour:* His servant, Crispin, announces in his inane way: "We have come to marry her . . . my master to take her to be his wife, I to have her as my mistress" (T I, 498). With Monsieur Argante's consent, Eraste will pretend to be a friend of his, so that he can give Mademoiselle Argante her full freedom of choice. In this manner he finds out that she plans to play the idiot to preserve her freedom. Love at first sight triumphs before Eraste's identity is clear to her.

The scenes where Mademoiselle Argante falls in love with Eraste are tender and delicate; in opposing her father she shows herself forthright and resolute: "One does not force a heart! That is the law! If you want to force mine, you break the law!" (T I, 497). She will not have a husband imposed on her and expresses herself in strong and picturesque terms. The young nobleman who is to come from the country, she calls "a nasty faun . . . an uncouth bear emerging from his den," and asks her father whether he takes her to be a "stupid monkey" (T I, 496-97).

To this hearty humor Master Pierre adds his bit. He claims "to govern" Monsieur Argante (T I, 484). First he sympathizes with Dorante whom Mademoiselle Argante thought she loved before she met Eraste; later he is all in favor of Eraste who pays him well. Master Pierre takes the place of Arlequin in the plays for the Italian troupe and does much to sustain the fun. He upbraids Monsieur Argante because he wants to marry his daughter to a nobleman (Eraste is noble, Dorante is not): "Noble blood? What the devil of an invention is that? How can blood flow in two ways when it all comes from the same river?" (T I, 484), but for all that, he will be happy to accept Eraste, once he has seen him. And then there is Crispin, naïve and funny. When Monsieur Argante asks whether the women can overhear them, he replies: "Gosh, Sir, you don't know women's ears. You see, those ears hear what one says half a mile away, and what one is going to say a quarter mile away" (T I, 498).

As compared to Molière, Dancourt, or Regnard, Marivaux' originality lies in the "surprise of love" which brings about the solution. Sentiment wins out: It leaves the audience almost stunned. What could be less unforeseen than the marriage that was long planned and that everyone expected?

IX   L'Ile des Esclaves
(The Island of Slaves),
comedy in one act, T. I., 1725.

Three island plays, *The Island of Slaves, The Island of Reason* (1727), and *The New Colony* (1729, published as *La Colonie,* 1750), continue the series of allegories that began with *L'Amour et la Vérité.* Delisle de la Drévetière had popularized the style through his *Arlequin Sauvage (Wild Harlequin),* 1721, a play that made daring attacks against injustice.

On the island of slaves, masters must trade places with their servants and undergo a course in humility (T I, 509). They are to gain perspective on the duties which accompany the privileges of rank and education. Arlequin says: "I shall be a bit insolent now I am the master" (T I, 530), and reminds Iphicrate that he used to call him "Hey, there!" as if he had no name (T I, 520). "Once you have suffered a little, you will become more reasonable and realize what suffering you may inflict on others!" (T I, 519). It is similar to *La Double Inconstance,* where Arlequin protests: "Dishonorable men are unworthy of being honored" with respect (T I, 272).

Euphrosine is subjected by Cléanthis, her maid, to the same reeducation, but the lesson is tempered, since a "naturally weaker sex" cannot avoid certain foibles (T I, 523, 531, cf. OD, 344). Marivaux has been called an outstanding spokesman for the equality of the sexes, but there are limitations to what equality he would recognize. Thus, Euphrosine is naturally flirtatious and vain. She loves beautiful clothes and the alluring négligées (T I, 527).[4] Cléanthis and Arlequin treat their masters with great kindness. They condemn overbearing and injustice, but sympathy takes the upper hand as soon as they have overcome their resentment (T I, 521). They do all they can to achieve a reconciliation. This makes the play both moving and effective.

Arlequin suggests that he revert to the service of his master (T I, 539), while Cléanthis feels for her mistress: In her servitude, "she has only her despair to keep her company" (T I, 537). Cléanthis started out by asserting her rights: "It is evil to base your merit on gold, silver, and rank alone" (T I, 540), but the plight of Euphrosine moves her to tears.

Marivaux is no revolutionary! Once the rights of the "slaves" have been clarified, they resume their former functions, while the noble Athenians are pardoned and may return home. Henceforth they will be aware of the demands of humanity; their natural goodness transcends their faults.

X   L'Héritier du Village
(The Farmer Inherits a Fortune),
comedy in one act, T.I., 1725.

Marivaux had portrayed peasants before, in *Pharsamon;* the *Télémaque Travesti;* Master Pierre is important in *Le Dénouement Imprévu;* soon Dimas, the gardener in *Le Triomphe de l'Amour,* will be added. However, in *L'Héritier du Village,* for the first time a character like Blaise, a farmer-would-be-gentleman, plays the main role. His good humor in wealth and poverty make for the success of the play.

Blaise has inherited a fortune, though it remains in the hands of a banker in the capital. Blaise aims to convert his family into high society. He will no longer be so foolish as to love his wife. His son, Colin, and his daughter, Colette, are to marry into nobility. Blaise is about to accept two penniless scoundrels as his children-in-law, Madame Damis and the Chevalier. Under these circumstances, news from Paris that bankruptcy has ruined him and wiped out his inheritance, is a blessing. It makes the two swindlers withdraw in haste. Colin and Colette will be all the happier and Blaise can settle down to enjoy the wine he ordered for the marriage feast.

Like *La Fausse Suivante,* the play does not end with happy marriages. On the contrary, here two very bad ones have been avoided. Like Silvia in *La Fausse Suivante,* Colin and Colette have escaped unhappiness, while Blaise can return to normalcy. Definitely, surprises of love do not triumph every time in Marivaux. Common sense wins out. Behind the gaiety, there is the realization that honor, nobility, and respectability can be shams. This is the theme on which Marivaux elaborates in his next journal, presenting the "indigent philosopher," his "philosophical bum."

Humor in *L'Héritier du Village* is rather sparse. There are few funny scenes besides one reminiscent of the *Spectateur.* As an aspiring member of the aristocracy, Blaise refuses to pay a bill; the tax collector has to fool him and make him believe that he is borrowing money, in order to get Blaise to settle his account (T I, 569). Marivaux must have noticed that gaiety was leaving him; the *Indigent Philosophe* seems like a determined effort to recapture it.

XI   L'Indigent Philosophe
(The Indigent Philosopher),
periodical in 7 issues, 1727.

A modern Diogenes except for his barrel, far from Paris and its hypocrisy, is drinking with a friend, the son of a drunken musician, and listens to his life story, a varied career which eventually turned him into a tragic actor, not a good one, but a good-looking one. As such he became the prize for whom vie two ladies of provincial society, two *précieuses ridicules;* he stands between "two vanities" (OD, 300). He derives great satisfaction from being desired even by such supercilious creatures. The story of this friend takes up somewhat less than half the periodical; his attitudes coincide closely with those of the philosophical bum himself. They share the haphazard view of life. After praising the virtues of wine, the friend says: "Your hat off, please, in spite of my ragged clothing" (OD, 295); the main character, in an analogous passage, significantly placed at the very end of the text, explains: I may be good, generous, easily forgiving, "but don't humiliate me" (OD, 323). A proud independence, a fierce individualism, a self-righteous insistence on their fundamental honesty qualifies the image of the two easy-going drinking companions significantly.

Our indigent philosopher is poor because he has spent the money he inherited; he dislikes his restricted means but he prefers the "ruinous follies" that have brought him there to the "sad follies" of those who think they are wise (OD, 280). He would gladly live his youth over again and reduce himself once again to poverty. If he had more money, he would spend it all. Worldly possessions hardly matter to him, only the enjoyment of life.

Another issue he seeks to make quite clear. He is fundamentally opposed to the reasonable attitudes of those who are considered serious, good citizens. He will have nothing to do with pedants, and let us recall that Marivaux repeatedly portrays *philosophes* as pedants. We shall find them described that way in the next two plays, *L'Ile de la Raison* and *La Seconde Surprise de l'Amour* and, for that matter, all the "Ancients" pictured in the previous works have similar traits. This sets "the philosophical bum" at opposite poles not only from rationalists of the traditional mold, but also from those who will eventually form around the *Encyclopédie*. It is characteristic that our philosopher admits he always was favorable to religion (OD, 318), though he also protests against excesses of "tender spirituality" (OD, 296-97) and laughs with a farmer who doubts that there is a soul because he never saw one (OD, 318). Yes, life must be laughter and he will drink water only if wine is not available (OD, 278), but there are fascinating aspects to this double opposition to the old-style and new-style *philosophes*. Marivaux seems to anticipate Carl Becker's *Heavenly City of Eighteenth Century Philosophers*, (Yale University Press, 1932), for he rejects the intransigent rationalism of many contemporaries, be they Aristotelians, orthodox "Ancients," or modern materialists. Becker felt that Voltaire and medieval philosophers shared a systematic intransigence. Marivaux condemns it at every step, most effectively perhaps in the most unsystematic *Indigent Philosophe*.

Our hero is naturally opposed to the show of wealth. He protests, as had the *Spectateur*, against resplendent clothes. The suit of one rich gentleman can provide the dowry of half a dozen orphans (OD, 307). He tells how a suitor was rejected because he was too simply dressed; when he came into money, he haughtily rejected the girl who now was anxious to marry him (OD, 319). Even more biting is the account of the young girl who married an old man for his wealth. She found the union ever so disappointing; she had never considered the natural failures of age (OD, 320).

There are bitter words, perhaps too bitter to suit the tone of the periodical, against evil persons *(les méchants)* who abuse their prerogatives (OD, 304-5), those who succeed because of family connections which should give them no rights other than to be known as the children of their parents (OD, 303). "How I hate them, how I detest them," he exclaims, though realizing that "we must live with everyone" and "pretend not to notice the impositions" of vanity (OD, 315). As elsewhere, Marivaux comes close to revolt but acquiesces: The reasonable man will feel only pity for false pride (OD, 309). Individuals and nations yearn for freedom, and are ready to die for it, but they would renounce complete independence were it granted because they would feel deprived of guidance and accuse those relinquishing control of being unconcerned with the welfare of the people (OD, 321); what attitude could be more conservative?

The indigent philosopher keeps coming back to the issue of vanity. He pretends to be happy without means just like Blaise, in *L'Héritier du Village,* after he lost his fortune. Our philosopher pretends to be content with the simple life and claims, "those who love joy have no vanity" (OD, 276), but later he contradicts all this: "Is there anything as malicious and lacking in humanity as vanity offended" (OD, 323). Men may act like children when they play with polite manners as with a hobby horse (OD, 323) but all men have their vanity, even those who hide it playfully:

We are all spirits of contradiction. As long as we can choose, we manifest no great desires. As soon as we have chosen our course, we want everything! If we made a good choice, we tire of it. What to do? If we are badly off, we want something better. When we obtain it, are we satisfied? Of course not! What is the solution? Everyone must search for it on his own." (OD, 321)

So he wants more than his humble existence! Our philosopher ends his account with the shrill warning: "Don't humiliate me!" (OD, 323).

When he pretended that his only objective in writing was "to be amusing" (OD, 317), was he not discounting his fierce pride? And how amusing is it to attack wealth, vanity and vain-glory, and to accuse evil persons of not even being human, because they are not humane and kind! (OD, 304). We sense a great deal of disillusionment and pessimism when we read: The good man, the gentleman, is "that creature you always want to deal with and would like to find in all parts, though you do not wish to be like him," the implication being that the good man always loses out (OD, 309). If we examine the text closely, we find the same accents of bitterness that qualify the previous works and made Marivaux create a character like Frédéric in *Le Prince Travesti.* The philosophical bum is lighthearted, he drinks; does he choose this front because he is so disillusioned?

XII *L'Ile de la Raison*
(The Island of Reason),
comedy in 3 acts, T. F., 1727

Gulliver's Travels had just been translated by the abbé Desfontaines when Marivaux staged his "little men" at the *Théâtre Français.* Obviously they had something to do with Swift. The translation had created a wave of interest. Marivaux was taking advantage of it, but even so these characters who change size one or several times were hard to put across. The play did not succeed.

A group of shipwrecked Europeans is reduced to diminutive size until they recover their reason, which means, until they understand their overbearing attitudes and are able to correct them. Marivaux insists his play is original (T I, 593) and he is right. His interpretation of reason is quite novel, his imitation of Swift is remote. We readily understand that he was not anxious to advertise a translation by his most biased critic. Marivaux' theme is that "one needs a great deal of judgment to realize one lacks judgment" (T I, 594). This implies that there is some hope of reform, a hope not germane to Swift's black pessimism. Marivaux' "animals" are nowhere as degenerate as those in Swift and his attack is more limited; it is directed against vanity and pride which prevent men from respecting the feelings of others. The humaneness demanded in the *Indigent Philosophe* is central also here.

The Europeans are all reduced in size upon landing; they recover their original size, i.e., their human greatness and dignity, at very different speeds. As in the Scriptures, the last shall be first. The servants, less tied to social prejudice, less in need to justify privilege, are first to become "reasonable." There is Blaise who will be a great help to Blectrue, the islander in charge of reeducating the group;[5] then comes Lisette who will also assist Blectrue; she guides her mistress, the Countess, toward seeing the light. The Countess has spent all too much

time on "the architecture of her hair," and on related foibles of vanity
(T I, 627-28). Frontignac, the Gascon secretary (cf. *Le Petit-Maître
Corrigé*) of the Courtier, also makes rapid progress and then can be a
model for his master.

The greatest difficulty is experienced by the three intellectuals in the
group. The Doctor must work hard to realize that he has considered
only his own enrichment. The Poet understands his faults, but soon
finds that he derives so much joy from attacking others by writing
poisonous little poems, that he relapses to small size. The Philosophe is
worse. He seems entirely incapable of becoming "great," so sure is he of
himself, so vain, so adamant. He will not concede anything. Blectrue
and the islanders will leave nothing undone to further the progress of
the Poet and the Philosophe (T I, 648). While this shows a fundamental
belief in human goodness, in man's capacity for regeneration, nothing is
said about how long it might take. It is interesting to note that Voltaire
could be designated in both cases; the two problem cases are left under
guard like Voltaire in the Bastille before he left for England. There is
nothing to confirm this association, but it is clear that Marivaux
advocates a kind of "reason" which is diametrically opposed to the
thought of Voltaire, a "reason of the heart" which makes him a
forerunner of Rousseau.

As on the island of slaves, the humanitarian ideal applies equally to
servants and to masters. To emphasize that the new society lacks all
prejudice, two islanders, Parmenès and Floris, the son and daughter of
the Governor, will marry two of the Europeans. The third marriage will
be that of Blaise and Lisette. Blaise continues to be the center of things
and has the most important part.

There are two revolutionary aspects to marriage on the island:
Women, recognized to be the weaker sex, are required to be first to
declare their love—this for their own protection (T I, 652-53)—and
marriage contracts are unnecessary since, once love is declared,
"reasonable" persons are in accord (T I, 648). These provisions
scandalized some readers. They are much in line with earlier statements
of Marivaux on these matters. In the last scene, the three marriages are
consecrated without contract, but in a formal ceremony before the
Governor.

One passage, the confession of the Poet, is important because it
elucidates, amusingly, Marivaux' theory of drama. The Poet tells that he
wrote both tragedies and comedies, and when Blectrue asks him to
explain what these genres represent, he says: In tragedy, the heroes

are so tender, alternately so admirably virtuous and so passionate, noble-criminals with such astonishing pride, whose crimes betray such greatness and whose self-accusations are so magnanimous, men, in short, with such respectable weaknesses, whom we admire for killing themselves at times in so noble a manner, that we cannot watch them without emotion and weeping for pleasure. (T I, 610)

Blectrue would prefer to see men weep over their faults, not over their virtues. The faults, the Poet explains, are pictured in the comedies, but they cause the spectators to laugh. This upsets Blectrue even more: "They laugh where they should weep?" Marivaux calls for a new genre which combines the serious with the burlesque, nobility of sentiment with the realism of traditional comedy.

The play failed. It was withdrawn after four performances. Only in 1950 did a director think of a simple device, a lift behind a bush, which could raise the Europeans, or lower them, from one stage to another, so as to simulate the large and the small stature. That performance, by the amateur troupe, L'Equipe, was the first successful one for this comedy.[6] Marivaux was evidently discouraged, and commented that he had been carried away by a unique situation incapable of staging (T I, 590); he was merely ahead of his time.

The Italian troupe honored the play with a parody, *L'Ile de la Folie (The Island of Folly)* by Dominique and Romagnesi (1727). It echoes Marivaux' themes. Reason is defined as that "little nothing" *(bagatelle)* which we acquire by simply giving away wealth, ridding ourselves of pride, prejudice, and malice, and by replacing these faults by candor, docility, and wisdom *(Parodies* IV, 147). Folly announces that Reason is threatened by a usurper, True Reason. We also find erotic fantasies. An island girl will first marry a Frenchman, then Gulliver the next day, because she knows Frenchmen are unfaithful; her plan will enable her "to enjoy all the pleasures of infidelity" *(Parodies,* IV, 171). The parody is no more of an attack on Marivaux than his own *Télémaque Travesti* was an attack on Fénelon. The Italian troupe remained on the best of terms with Marivaux. On April 22, 1728, they will perform his *Triomphe de Plutus.*

XIII   La (Seconde) Surprise de l'Amour
(The (Second) Surprise of Love),
comedy in 3 acts, T. F., 1727.

The "indigent philosopher" was above all anxious to free himself from the fetters of society and give himself over to his subjective sensibility. In a somewhat more somber mood, this applies also to the two principal characters of Marivaux' new *Surprise de l'Amour,* written so that the *Théâtre Français* would also have a play on this theme in its repertoire; as usual there were difficulties and a considerable delay between submission of the script and performance.

The Chevalier formerly loved Angélique; she was forced to join a convent in order not to accept the husband her parents wanted to impose on her. The Marquise is recently widowed and as disillusioned with marriage and society as the Chevalier. They have foresworn the world for six months and quite literally buried themselves in their grief. The Chevalier will "steep himself in sorrow until death"; the Marquise agrees that this has been her very thought. They are ever so sensitive (T I, 683) and realize that their meeting is a unique experience, "the only tolerable moment in these difficult times" (T I, 684).

They understand their plight and each other, but they are utterly deluded in believing that their meeting of minds can limit itself to a mere "friendship" *(amitié),* to a feeling of solidarity between two persons disappointed in love (T I, 686). In her treatise on friendship, Mme de Lambert had stressed how difficult it was to establish such a relationship between members of the opposite sex. In view of this, it is most amusing to find the Marquise mention this *Traité de l'Amitié* to Hortensius as a book she has enjoyed (T I, 698). Hortensius is the pedant she has engaged to edify her and bring her the consolation of philosophy. He spouts useless syllogisms and tries to seduce Lisette; he is the very image of the ridiculous *philosophe.*

It will take three acts and a plan for the Marquise to marry the Count (it almost entraps her) to make her love for the Chevalier apparent. They engage in self-pity and much sentiment. The scenes with Hortensius are hilarious and make up for this. They are determined to go their separate ways, but when they meet "a last time" to say goodbye, the "surprising effects of sympathy" bring them just that much closer to each other; their case is unique, and a unique love must lead to marriage (T I, 683, n. 14).

In this play obstacles are internal, for the Chevalier is free to make his decisions and the Marquise is a young widow with the enviable advantage of being able to arrange her future as only widows could. The plot draws on sources not only in Marivaux' own work, but on some of the oldest and most traditional like the *Matron of Ephesus* (who set out to mourn her dead husband and before long was willing to abandon even his corpse to save the soldier she loved and kept from guarding a hanged man), recently restaged by La Motte. *La Surprise* is an excellent play, less successful than it should have been because the French troupe did not have the actors to do it justice; there was no one like Thomassin-Arlequin of the Italian players; for the same reason Blaise, in *L'Île de la Raison,* had not appeared as comic as he was intended to be. To make the meeting of two disappointed persons, isolated in their loneliness, a subject for comedy, requires resources of superior sensitiveness and talent. Modern performances have been most successful.

XIV   Le Triomphe de Plutus
(Plutus Triumphant),
comedy in 1 act, T. I., 1728.

This farce of "bourgeois mythology" (Jean Fabre) comes to life through the character of Plutus. He appears as Monsieur Richard (Rich Man) and resolves to win the girl whom Apollo-Ergaste is courting with his good looks and delicate sentiments. The victory of Plutus is complete. He captures the love of Aminte, he obtains the cooperation of her uncle, Armidas, of Spinette, her maid, and even of Arlequin, the valet of Ergaste, for Plutus has money at his disposal, not just pretty words; those of Ergaste seem quite shopworn at that. Plutus' final triumph comes when he takes over the musicians whom Ergaste has hired. The audience is all for him, as well, since Apollo's initial self-confidence was full of conceit. Apollo grasps none of his mistakes and bitterly accuses the fate which permitted that the God of wealth should take precedence over the God of merit.

The play furnishes one of the most eloquent proofs that Marivaux is not to be identified—as all too often he has been—with the unworldly, abstract, and hopeless *bel-esprit* Apollo represents. The plays without happy endings, like *La Fausse Suivante, L'Héritier du Village,* and characterizations in other plays and essays from the earliest to the *Indigent Philosophe* have caused us to speak of Marivaux' realism. Allegorical setting, the use of stock characters, and other self-imposed restrictions never infringe on the individuality of his portrayals. They involve desire, sensuality, vanity, greed, love of rank and power, and every other fault unreconcilable with the excessive delicacy that many critics attributed to him. Ever since Marivaux showed Truth taking refuge in a well to poison its waters *(L'Amour et la Vérité),* he has expressed his conviction that the forces of life win out over the kind of spirituality which makes one yawn (OD, 296). Plutus is the life-force;

one must cope with him. There may have been times when Marivaux wished that he were more like him!

CHAPTER 5

Plays and Novels of the Prime.

I   Le Jeu de l'Amour et du Hasard
(The Game of Love and Chance),
comedy in 3 acts, T. I., 1730.

IT had been five years since Marivaux had written a role for Silvia. The actress had not been well in 1726, and often absent, as when the *Triomphe de Plutus* was performed. Her return made *Le Jeu de l'Amour* a success from the start, deservedly so, for it is remarkable for its brilliant repartee and structural simplicity.

Silvia and Dorante are destined for each other by their parents, but only if they are in accord. In order to observe the other better and make sure they are made for each other, each of them, independently, decides to trade places with a servant. Silvia's father, Monsieur Orgon, and her brother, Mario, are aware of the plans and highly amused; they decide not to interfere. In their disguise, the couples fall in love exactly as they should, for the superior sensitivity of the masters and the good-natured humor and burlesque bearing of Lisette and Arlequin establish a distinction, in sensitivity, not just in rank, which raises an absolute barrier. Silvia abhors Arlequin and loves Dorante. She even finds herself arguing with Lisette to defend Dorante and becoming angry with her; she cannot understand why (T I, 821), while Arlequin had seemed outrageous and repulsive to her ever since his arrival, ever since he boldly asked for his father-in-law, saying he came to marry and might as well call him that (T I, 811-12).

Dorante, who imagines that he is in love with a servant, is close to despair. He decides to return home, but in one last conversation with Silvia he will tell her his identity. As in the second *Surprise de l'Amour,* the farewell becomes the realization of a great love. In the most moving moments of the play, Silvia reacts to his revelation with an aside: "Ah, now I understand my heart," and adds, when Dorante has gone: "How important it was for me that he be Dorante" (T I, 829-30).

Without her feminine vanity, Silvia would have admitted who she

[67]

was and the play would have ended with the second act, but she prefers to challenge her lover to the supreme sacrifice; she wants Dorante's offer to marry her in her lowly condition! To continue the comedy on her own terms, she obtains the assent of Monsieur Orgon and of Mario; they do feel she is pushing the young man too far but are willing to go along once again.

The fairy prince, in *La Double Inconstance,* married a simple subject of his; the Prince of Leon, in *Le Prince Travesti,* was willing to marry Hortense; the islanders of *L'Ile de la Raison* did not disdain Europeans; now Silvia asks an even greater sacrifice of Dorante, for if he is wrong in assuming that his father will accept Silvia as soon as he sets eyes on her (T I, 844), he will have forfeited his inheritance for a servant girl—or so it seems.

Still, Silvia succeeds. Only when Dorante has promised eternal faithfulness—"he will never change!"—does she tell Dorante who her father is. Does Dorante regret his anguish? No, he is happy to have given such admirable proof of his true intentions (T I, 845). His suffering during the action must not be underestimated: it is the hallmark of a noble soul!

Fortunately we have the hilarious parallel of Arlequin and Lisette. She realizes that she has lit a fire in the man she takes to be Dorante and cannot believe her ears when Monsieur Orgon tells her to go right ahead, in spite of this (T I, 815). There are funny scenes: Once Arlequin, once Lisette, are forced to listen to their master or mistress even though they are supposed to have all the prerogatives. Finally Arlequin is required to confess to Lisette that he is not the noble "captain" she thought he was, but only a "soldier in his captain's anteroom." Lisette takes it in good grace because, as she puts it, she is merely Silvia's hairdresser. They readily forgive and are ready to marry.

There is something paradoxical about these two couples who wear masks in order to discover the truth. The fact that Arlequin normally wears a black face mask makes this even funnier. But then we have already found the Truth hiding at the bottom of a well; the truth is elusive and of many faces; Marivaux' name is frequently mentioned as a precursor of Pirandello.

The other remarkable aspect of the play is the assumption of a hierarchy of souls; on each level there are kindred spirits made for each other. The loyalty and good will of the servants does not suffice to make them into masters. They cannot impersonate them successfully. The servants in *L'Ile des Esclaves* felt this just as strongly. Marivaux establishes degrees of sensitivity which parallel distinctions of rank.

Dorante and Silvia could not lapse into servant mentality, just as Marianne, in the novel, could not hide her noble soul. It is their true distinction. In this way the masks, ultimately, add to their freedom and self-expression.

II   La Vie de Marianne
(The Life of Marianne),
novel in 11 parts:
I: 1731; II: 1734; III: 1735; IV-VI: 1736;
VII: 1737; VIII: 1738; IX-XI: 1741.

In 1728, the *Spectateur* first appeared in book form; that same year, Marivaux obtained authorization *(privilège)* to publish *La Vie de Marianne* where he might apply his techniques of analysis and reflection to the description of a single heroine. It can be said that, in so doing, he created the modern psychological novel, though there might be some justification for honoring *La Princesse de Clèves* of Mme de Lafayette with this distinction. It can hardly be attributed to Samuel Richardson, for it is now established that he knew *Marianne* when he wrote *Pamela:* He worked for Davis, the publisher of the English translation of *Marianne,* the year its first two volumes came out; he either set its type or used it as a model.

Marivaux was quite aware of his innovations. He explains: "An exact portrait as I promised you is an endless task" (M, 227). The first three parts, composed over seven years, describe only three days in Marianne's life. He never escaped the witticism of his critic, Desfontaines, that he would never catch up with her progress; even in later years, when Marivaux increased the tempo of composition, he never covered as much time as it took him to write the novel: He portrayed 7 weeks in Parts IV-V, 6 in Part VII, 2 days in Part VIII, and in the last three parts Marianne listens to Tervire's story which could be told in a few days.

Clearly, he did not undertake to be an historian, but an analyst of thought and feelings; what mattered were motives, ideas. When critics blamed him for exaggerating distinctions, for being precious, or incomprehensible, he redefined his literary purpose in *Le Cabinet du Philosophe* (1734) and said: "New words, new signs are needed to express the new ideas shared by our generation" (OD, 383). It was the most direct attack yet against traditional principles of rhetoric and a vocabulary sanctioned by purists who admitted only the words in the dictionary of the French Academy. The modern reader finds nothing

incomprehensible; he is not shocked by the "neologisms" that bothered
Desfontaines because they have all become accepted; he is even less
worried about the scene that caused cries of outrage, the insults of a
laundress, Madame Dutour, and of the coachman who, she thought, was
overcharging Marianne (at the end of Part II). "Unworthy of a refined
mind," said Desfontaines (M, lxviii), but the realism is very mild for
modern ears. The attacks explain why Marivaux shifted to writing the
Paysan Parvenu in 1734, and why he denied authorship of the
Télémaque Travesti, entirely conceived in burlesque terms, when it
appeared, against his will, in 1736.

Marianne is a foundling, taken in by a country priest when thieves
killed all other passengers of a stagecoach. It is carefully noted,
however, that these included footmen, for this vouches for Marianne's
noble birth. By the time she is fifteen and a half, she finds herself in
Paris. Her foster father and his sister, who brought her to the capital,
have died. She appeals for help to Father Saint-Vincent. Unwittingly
the latter throws her into the arms of a religious hypocrite, a Tartuffe,
Monsieur de Climal. Marianne understands his motives far more rapidly
than she is willing to admit, for she profits from his aid and his
presents. It is only when he wants to move her from the home of
Madame Dutour to a "small house" in the country, kept by a woman
who has his confidence, where he will be able to visit her secretly, that
she decides his course will ruin her reputation and future. It is then that
she breaks with him, decides to return all gifts, and explains: "One no
longer has principles when one makes others hope one has none" (M,
48).

The entire account is that of Marianne as a fifty-year-old dowager,
wealthy, who must have come into money through marriage, and intent
on making herself look virtuous. She sees it to her advantage to tell how
naïve she was in her youth, but had she really been naïve, would she
have known the last possible moment to escape Climal's clutches? It is
characteristic that her stated principle of moral qualms is utterly
ambiguous; the reader must not be seduced by her eloquent and clever
protestations. Marianne is remarkably, even dangerously articulate.

Marianne now returns to Father Saint-Vincent. She attempts to
overcome his almost incredible innocence, but he will not believe his
ears. Unsure of where to go, she enters the chapel of a convent, to weep
and meditate. Most fortunately for her, she is overheard by Madame de
Miran, by coincidence the sister of Monsieur de Climal, the very image
of kindness. She takes pity on Marianne and pays her way into the

convent. Valville, the son of Madame de Miran, has been madly in love with Marianne ever since the day he saw her leaving church and twisting her ankle. She described this as a welcome circumstance, which allowed the young man to look at it in all decency (M, 67). The greatest problem was to return home without having Valville find out the mortifying circumstance that she lived with Madame Dutour, a laundress; it is for this reason she took a coach, and this precipitated the argument between the coachman and Madame Dutour upon arrival (M, 92-94).

Thus, for having followed the path of virtue and left Climal, Marianne has not only found a kind lady who will treat her like a mother and help her financially—the convent would not have considered her without the entrance fee—but she has moved closer to the man she loves; it is the first instance in which Marivaux counters the lack of luck in his own life by having virtue rewarded in cash. It is, of course, an ironical element, particularly in view of Marianne's deviousness, for she had not followed her resolve to the letter: She was still wearing the prettiest dress Climal had given her, better to impress Father Saint-Vincent and others, Madame de Miran, for instance, and the abbess of the convent.

Marianne harbors no illusions and, for love of Madame de Miran, offers to renounce ever marrying Valville. She knows that a foundling cannot easily pretend to such a match and that the only way of succeeding is to pretend renunciation. After all, this is a Christian virtue, most attractive in itself, and likely to provide means where no direct approach would. Marianne seems to make a series of noble sacrifices, but she is always amply rewarded. It is difficult, if not impossible, to disentangle her motives, selfless or self-seeking, mostly both at the same time. We shall find the same ambiguity and implied irony in the portrait of Jacob, her male counterpart in the *Paysan Parvenu,* only Marianne is more subtle, coy, and feminine; the way she tells it, she is as virtuous as cultured and delicate; but close examination of her actions does not bear this out.

The admirable character of Madame de Miran (M, 167-72) is the portrait of Madame de Lambert who died in 1733. It is a tribute to her, a debt of friendship from Marivaux who benefited so greatly from her help and the acquaintances made in her salon. Her close friend, whom he introduces soon thereafter, Madame Dorsin (M, 210-30), is Madame de Tencin whose salon he frequented henceforth and who was to organize the support for his election to the French Academy in 1742. Both of these ladies aid Marianne a great deal. Eventually they even agree to her marriage with Valville. Matters are not so simple, however; they cannot shield the girl from the wrath of relatives who will not hear of such an alliance.

The relatives have Marianne abducted from the convent. She is treated like a prisoner in another, and finally brought before the minister (he is the portrait of Fleury)[1] who will attend a family council and listen to the conflicting pleas, including that of Madame de Miran. Marianne's self-defense is a triumph. She has talked well before; here she outdoes herself. Once again she renounces all plans of marrying Valville and thus annihilates the opposition, but she opposes with equal vigor an alternative plan proposed by the minister, her marriage to the uninspiring and lowly Villot. In fact, she not only escapes Villot, a poor fellow who has nothing to say, but she manages to preserve her freedom; she need not, as had originally been decided, choose between Villot and permanent vows in a convent. The minister is most impressed: "How can we keep virtue from being attractive" (M, 337), he concludes. Indeed, Marianne is infinitely attractive. Only the most obstinate and sour of the relatives will not concede the point, and this includes the two ladies who organized her abduction.

The novel could now end happily, but as Marivaux stated in the *Cabinet du Philosophe:* "The fastest way to kill love is to satisfy it" (OD, 338). No one will deny Valville to a girl of such noble sentiment, capable of such admirable renunciation speeches, but Valville now lacks obstacles that tie him to her; it is all too easy. One day he encounters an attractive girl in Marianne's convent, Mademoiselle Varthon. She has just fainted and her corset has to be loosened. This sight is as overwhelming for Valville as had been his first glance at Marianne's ankle. Mademoiselle Varthon is cooperative. She confides in Marianne, she shows her his letter, she gives up all claims to marrying him, but Marianne knows better. Mademoiselle Varthon is not responsible for being so attractive; Marianne has won much herself by pretending to step back. Besides, as Marivaux explains, Valville is no monster of ingratitude, merely "a man, a Frenchman, the typical contemporary of the suitors of our time" (M, 376). In the face of the fickleness of fate, Marianne ponders whether she should become a nun. This is why she listens to the story of Tervire (Parts IX-XI). Tervire has joined the religious life, but she warns Marianne not to give up the world too readily. It is quite possible that Marivaux' daughter was considering a convent as early as 1741 and that he was also talking to her.

Tervire's story is melodramatic and bitter. Her father was disowned for marrying her mother. When he dies, her mother remarries in Paris and leaves the girl to neighbors in the country. Tervire is relatively happy staying with a farmer, Villot (Marivaux is indifferent to names; he does not care about the coincidence in name with the man Marianne at one time was to marry), but she soon falls under the influence of Madame de Sainte-Hermières. This creature of intrigue is looking for a ready solution to rid herself of her obligation to Tervire's mother. She works on Tervire to become a nun. When the results are negative, she wants to marry her to the elderly Monsieur de Sercour. Then Madame de Sainte-Hermières falls in with the abbé, Sercour's nephew, who wants his uncle's inheritance for himself and presumably will pay off Madame de Sainte-Hermières for her assistance. For this reason, they organize a frame-up, to ruin Tervire's reputation in the eyes of Sercour. The abbé is found, at night, in her closet and a compromising letter (she wrote it innocently from dictation) used to prove that she invited him. The plan succeeds, Sercour gives up Tervire; only the deathbed confession of Madame de Sainte-Hermières clears Tervire's name, but at a time when Sercour is no longer interested in her. Marivaux likes such scenes of confession: Climal, likewise, waited until just before his death to admit his evil schemes to Father Saint-Vincent and to his family, and endow Marianne with a modest income, though larger than what he would have given her to become his mistress.

Meanwhile, a relative, Madame Dursan, has moved into the area and taken in Tervire. One day a poacher is found in the woods. Madame Dursan seeks his punishment, but Tervire is full of sympathy because he is stealing for his family who are without food or resources. Eventually she manages to have Madame Dursan hire his wife as her maid. It is another of Marivaux' remarkable cases of coincidence. He turns out to be Madame Dursan's son, with whom she had broken over his marriage; she had sworn never to see him again. When she finally is told who he is, she is close to death. The touching scene of recognition brings relief. Repentance and tears make up for past anger and one more deathbed conversion instills kindness into the atmosphere of hate and violence.

Much of the melodrama in Tervire's life reminds us of Marivaux' first novel; the sarcasm of the abbé and the tenderness of the last moments in Madame Dursan's life are welcome diversions. After her death, the tone reverts to that of violence. Tervire travels to Paris in search of her mother; she finds her destitute, for she has bequeathed her fortune to her son from a second marriage and he does nothing to support her (cf. Balzac's *Père Goriot*). Tervire finds only his wife at home. She undertakes to upbraid her in a furious discourse, with sentences longer than any others in Marivaux' work (M, 577-79). The only response she elicits is irony: "You would make an excellent preacher" (M, 578). Such is the end of *La Vie de Marianne*. It terminates in utter frustration with an impotent discourse. The novel remains incomplete. We know, of course, that Tervire became a nun while Marianne married and acquired the means to live a life of ease. When she tells her story at the age of fifty, she says nothing of her husband. Continuators[2] have assumed that she married Valville. Marivaux is silent; why belabor the obvious?

The articulateness of Marivaux' heroines is noteworthy. Tervire's invective is as remarkable as Marianne's six discourses in self-justification, when she breaks with Climal (M, 121f), tries to convince Father Saint-Vincent that Climal is a Tartuffe (M, 139f), sells herself to Madame de Miran (M, 150f), tries, for her sake, to dissuade Valville from marrying her (M, 194f), speaks to the abbess detaining her (M, 298f), and to the minister who presides at the family council (M, 333f). Indeed, these speeches are increasingly important and culminate in her greatest triumph. By contrast, there is Marianne's conversation with Villot whom she will not marry; there, she purposely expresses herself "in monosyllables" (M, 308).

The richness of contrasting styles distinguishes the novel. In addition to the rhetoric and antirhetoric we have just noted, there are other moods: the language of passion which expresses itself in sobs and sighs, with many exclamations. According to Frédéric Deloffre,[3] it is used with more restraint than by more sentimental contemporaries, but it is strikingly different from other types of passages; then again there is spirited dialogue as in the plays, but with the additional resource of third-person comment.

Another element was much discussed and brought out with predilection by critics in Marivaux' day: Marianne's "reflections." They may be analytical or deluded, penetrating or deceitful. One example of her ambivalence, quoted earlier, is her statement that one must draw the line somewhere (with Climal), preferably before it is too late. Other illustrations show her capacity for introspection: "Our soul knows what it does," she admits, "instinct guides it" (M, 180). She speculates that "only our feelings yield reliable information about ourselves" (M, 22). Many times her thoughts complement those in the *Cabinet du Philosophe*, e.g., comments that self-interest and vanity are second nature. At one time Marianne criticizes a sermon: "Vaingloriously, the vanity of the objects of this world was being condemned" (M, 204). Even our loftiest aspirations are very much steeped in our ego! Frequently, the most important lesson, or commentary, is not what is stated, but what is implied; behind the articulateness there is a world of silence for the reader's consideration. Marianne, for instance, is called a "beautiful soul," but this does not keep her from weeping when it best suits her purposes. She does not only sob from tenderness or despair, but cleverly, and in her prettiest dress, to attract attention, as in the convent chapel after leaving Climal.

Objective accounts alternate with self-deception, passionate outbursts, sarcasm, bitterness, and tenderness or humor. Marivaux introduces a richness of tone and variety of style we do not find in his contemporaries. In *Manon Lescaut,* for instance, the abbé Prévost expresses every incident or emotion in the same pure language; he lacks contrast in form, if not in content. Marivaux' psychological investigation is far livelier. The style of each speaker and situation is determined by its unique purpose and setting. *La Vie de Marianne* is a most interesting novel, even if it is structurally less perfect than the simpler, shorter, perhaps more effective *Paysan Parvenu.*

III   La Réunion des Amours
(Two Kinds of Love Reconciled),
comedy in one act, T. F., 1731.

Marivaux' novels did not keep him from his other pursuits. In his long-standing struggle to succeed at the Comédie Française, he had submitted his longest and most subtle play, *Les Serments Indiscrets,* and since staging encountered obstacles, he presented *La Réunion des Amours* as an incidental short piece at the occasion of the second birthday of Crown Prince Louis; it was first to be performed. It takes up the opposition between tender and sensual love as we find them in *Le Triomphe de Plutus.* In *La Réunion des Amours,* Plutus associates with Cupid while Apollo supports the more tender and intellectual qualities of love.

The issue is: How to endow a young prince with all the desirable attributes. This is debated by Love and Cupid before Minerva (Sc. 10) and, after consulting with Truth, Minerva urges the two opponents to unite (T I, 876), for while Cupid may be too libertine and sensuous, Apollo is too tender and unrealistic. The prince should benefit from both.

There are amusing asides. Truth questions dedicatory epistles where authors rarely say what they think, for "persons truly praiseworthy are much scarcer than such epistles" (T I, 867). Then we hear that much of the poetry composed under the auspices of Apollo is insincere. Apollo is upset but Truth soon makes up with him and concedes that poets are men of wit *(gens d'esprit)* who "sooner or later become gentlemen" (T I, 868). The audience will take the compliment with several grains of salt for in *L'Ile de la Raison,* the Poet never succeeded!

These jokes are less pertinent that the comments of Cupid. Admittedly he was born without "the little formality" of marriage (T I, 872). He proclaims: "I give love . . . . I light the fire . . . for the benefit of the universe" (T I, 872); elsewhere he puts it more simply: "I give life" (T I, 863). In the *Spectateur,* Marivaux had protested against "love which is but a sigh" (OD, 206); tearful sentimentality, he felt, is an aberration. Cupid's sensuality is needed. When Love predicts that Cupid's reign will soon cease to exist (T I, 861), he is not only wrong, he is lost in the clouds like Apollo-Ergaste in *Le Triomphe de Plutus.* Cupid is clearly the author's favorite, though he must ultimately join forces with Love. Marivaux dislikes unrealistic social codes, the abstractions of stylized poetry (which make Apollo an "Ancient" not a "Modern"). He distrusts the utopian but, at the same time, pernicious schemes of those who pride themselves on wisdom, like Minerva, and think they can simply omit Cupid from the guest list (T I, 861); life will admit him anyhow!

IV   Le Triomphe de l'Amour
(The Triumph of Love),
comedy in 3 acts, T. I., 1732.

Romance and adventure make this play into an heroic comedy, much like *Le Prince Travesti.* It was a notable success like *La Fausse Suivante,* an excellent medium for Silvia who could reappear in male attire. Silvia's role is that of Léonide, Princess of Sparta, daughter of a usurper of the throne. Idealistically she sets out to marry the rightful heir to the kingdom, Agis. In this way she can restore him to power, but first she must deceive the guardians who watch over Agis: Hermocrate and his sister, Léontine, simple-minded and pedantic "philosophers" who are all too easily deceived. She succeeds in making both of them fall in love with her, Hermocrate in the disguise of Aspasie, Léontine in male attire, as Phocion. She manages to allay their misgivings, their fear of strangers above all, for no one had received their permission to approach Agis before. She convinces them that the great moment to love has come for the first time in their lives. At the same time she wins Agis.

Silvia displays inimitable skill as Cupid and Plutus all in one, but she is also tender love and, for that matter, power, for her guards have surrounded the estate and give her an easy means of triumph at the end. She has no difficulty paying off Arlequin and the gardener, Dimas, one of the best comic creations of Marivaux. She conquers with artifice, money, soldiers, also with idealism; she uses the mask but, most of all, her intelligence. Hermocrate and Léontine, who resemble Hortensius in the second *Surprise,* are no match for her.

Is she moral, reprehensible, credible in her role as a princess? These questions have preoccupied critics who found the plot complex, but the masterful staging by Jean Vilar (1955, 1967) has shown how irrelevent such worries are. Fantasy triumphs, the force of love puts philosophy to shame. Marivaux is still a "Modern" who imputes only sterile thoughts and sterile hearts to his opponents. As Léonide, princess of Sparta, Sylvia surpasses the deeds of many heroes of romance, but in a light-hearted, amusing atmosphere, with funny repartee. We only regret that we cannot quote this play at length.

V   Les Serments Indiscrets
(Oaths all too Rashly Taken),
comedy in 5 acts, T. F., 1732.

Marivaux' most ambitious comedy, the only one in five acts, though not much longer than the preceding one, had to wait fifteen months before the French troupe agreed to stage it. It never achieved success. It is, nonetheless, most interesting and Marivaux lists it among his preferred plays, perhaps because it failed, to prove he was right in not cutting it; he barely complied with the many requests to do so; he could be very stubborn.

The framework is that of *Le Dénouement Imprévu* and of *Le Jeu de l'Amour.* A reluctant young couple will marry according to their parents' choice, but they do not give in easily; they will decide of their own free will. There is a complication. Lucile and Damis commit themselves by mutual agreement not to get married. They do so at the prompting of Lisette. The fool-hardy resolution that gives the play its title, stands like a wall between them. They are foolish to "defy" each other's charms, especially when they know they are in love and have found so much in common (T I, 975-77, 993). Love at first sight upsets their well laid plans, but not until the end of five agonizing acts. They resist too long! Marivaux realizes it. Ever so often, he interjects exhortations to hurry, to bring matters to a close (T I, 971, 977, 978, 982, 994, 996, 999, 1002, 1003, 1017, 1025). There is some humor in this technique, but not enough comic relief to put the play over. For once Marivaux should have given in and shortened the action. He would not; on the contrary, he added an adament preface pointing out that the situation is unique, quite different from the *Surprises*. Voltaire found in the play "a lot of metaphysics and little that is natural" (T I, 961), but he was hardly interested in expressing appreciation. The play is fascinating, not effective.

Two elements are new: Damis picks on Lucile's sister, Phénice, to foil the parents' plan. The second innovation is the role of the servants, Lisette and Frontin. They set out to drive their masters apart instead of reflecting their desires.

The role of Phénice is interesting. She is in danger of becoming a toy, a tool like Rosette in Musset's *On ne Badine pas avec l'Amour (Don't Toy with Love)*, the play inspired by *Les Serments*. Phénice escapes Rosette's tragic fate only because she is a realist. She is neither fooled nor seduced by Damis' proposal; even before Frontin tells her, she knows Lucile and Damis love each other (T I, 1010). She plays the game and deceives Lucile right to the point of pretending to sign a contract to marry Damis. Thus she forces Lucile in the end to capitulate and take back her oath. All along, Phénice is sure Damis will not marry her, though she never discusses the issue with him.

Meanwhile, Lisette and Frontin develop the novel idea that they can control their masters better and receive more exclusive attentions or benefits from them if they keep them apart (T I, 983-84). It is only when Ergaste, the father of Damis, threatens to disinherit his son if he does not marry Phénice—for Damis keeps saying he loves Phénice and Ergaste is perfectly willing to accept her instead of Lucile, the original choice—that the servants give in. They see their financial futures threatened, like Dimas and Arlequin in *Le Triomphe de l'Amour*.

From that moment on, Lisette and Frontin reverse their objective. They work to bring Damis and Lucile together (T I, 999f), only this is not so simple. Lisette has lied to Lucile in saying that Phénice loves Damis; she has lied to Lucile's father, Orgon, about the same matter (T I, 977, 984, 986). All this must be undone; they are forced to enroll Phénice in their plan. For reasons difficult to explain, but no doubt very clear to Marivaux, Lucile not only respects her oath like a sacrament, but it is assumed that it is only up to her to break it, a little as in *L'Ile de la Raison*, where women must be the first to declare their love. Damis cannot break the impasse. And so the "quarrel of delicate feelings" (T I, 989) continues until Phénice pretends to sign a marriage contract with Damis, and Lucile is reduced to despair.

There is some humor. When Frontin tells Damis of his father's ultimatum, he says that it grants the wrong kind of freedom, a choice between Phénice and financial ruin (T I, 1001). There are the continuous reminders to hurry, which we have mentioned. There is the conclusion of Lucile that "our adventure will make people laugh, but our love makes up for this" (T I, 1028). There is just not enough comedy.

Some critics had suggested that *Les Serments* reenacted the two *Surprises de l'Amour.* It is against this unjust reproach that Marivaux directs his prefatory note. He points out that the two earlier plays present suitors in love without knowing it, while in *Les Serments,* they are aware of their love but have pledged not to heed it: "A great difference indeed; none could be more basic in matters of sentiment" (T I, 996). The question is, does the spectator attach as much importance to such distinctions as Marivaux, for in all cases there are couples in love who cannot talk about their affection. Marivaux' theory of analysis and unique situations justifies his point of view. Furthermore, he was proud of the modifications brought to his theater by *Les Serments.* It was a seminal play that changed the function of servants and introduced the pretended rivalry of a third person, so successfully employed in *L'Heureux Stratagème;* finally, it recast the whole question of personal commitment.

The first performance was interrupted by whistling and other noises. Five acts were too long for delaying a marriage without visible obstacles. Marivaux drew his lesson and incorporated his discoveries into later works.

VI L'Ecole des Mères
(A School for Mothers),
comedy in one act, T. I., 1732.

A title so close to *L'Ecole des Femmes (A School for Wives)* could not help but evoke Molière but, characteristically, Marivaux shied away from his style; his sources are rather Piron, *L'Ecole des Pères,* and Dancourt, *La Parisienne,* which even provided the four main characters (T II, 3-4). Once again Marivaux shows that he is aware that he cannot outdo the master in his own field.

Our heroine is Angélique, "an Agnès raised under strictest parental control" (T II, 15). She has fallen in love with Eraste, and this creates a burning desire for independence, for she knows there is a favored suitor; by coincidence, it is the father of Eraste, but this will not be known until later. The young couple do not aim to outwit the older generation; they will not elope; they want to obtain their parents' grudging consent.

Issues 12 and 16 of the *Spectateur* had proposed the need for communication between parents and children; a later play, *La Mère Confidente,* will carry the theme much further. Angélique defends herself extremely well, and Lisette helps. Angélique asks what would become of her if she had to submit to the will of a husband, age 60 (T II, 20), and her maid puts it more bluntly: Her virtue would be put to a severe test! (T II, 18) Does her mother think about such things? Does she understand at all? "My mother will protect me from evil, but does she know about it? She must have found out what it is! And so will I!" (T II, 21) She questions the value of abstract principles and discourses. Her call for experience is, of course, not without danger. She speculates:

I am by nature inclined to virtue, but do you realize that I fall asleep when I listen to lectures on good behavior? And are you so sure that I will be happy for having avoided all flirtations? I will, but it would serve my mother right if I engaged in love affairs. (T II, 22-23)

Madame Argante, her mother, and Orgon, Eraste's father disguised as Damis, better think about the dangers they face, for their plan of having Angélique marry Orgon is patently absurd.

The situation will be resolved with unprecedented speed at a masquerade ball. Eraste appears dressed like a servant, La Ramée, and Angélique tells that she loves him right to his face, not knowing, of course, who he is (T II, 24). Orgon cannot help giving in to his son, partly because he hears his son paying him the flattering compliment, quite undeserved, that he is a reasonable and understanding father (T II, 35). Madame Argante declares herself satisfied; Eraste marries Angélique.

The unusual haste is like an answer to critics who said *Les Serments Indiscrets* moved too slowly toward a solution. The dialogue is sprightly and funny. During the masquerade, Eraste flatters his father at the very moment he forces him to give up Angélique. The servants have reverted to the traditional pattern. Lisette marries Frontin, Champagne is rejected by Lisette just as Orgon is rufused by Angélique. The play was a rousing success. Once again, the Italian stage made up for failure with the French troupe.

VII   L'Heureux Stratagème
(The Lucky Stratagem),
comedy in 3 acts, T. I., 1733.

As usual, a long delay intervened before the performance of a play Marivaux had sent to the Comédie Française. *Le Petit-Maître Corrigé* was held up. Meanwhile, *L'Heureux Stratagème* became another major success for Silvia and the Italian troupe.

The love of the Countess for Dorante has grown stale; she is now flirting with the Chevalier to satisfy her vanity. Dorante is desperate and so is the Marquise whom the Chevalier has abandoned. The two disappointed lovers will band together; they will pretend love and are ready to carry their game right to the signing of a marriage contract. If their "stratagem" works, Dorante can be reunited with the Countess and the Marquise with the Chevalier. They act as if they have read *Les Serments Indiscrets* and hope the trick will work for them as well.

The high point is the confrontation between the Countess and the Marquise (T II, 75f), a most striking contrast: What is said bears little relation to their true feelings. The Marquise tells the Countess, ironically, that she is frankness personified; the Countess replies that the statement proves the Marquise is completely insincere. It is a battle of wits where every sentence is calculated for the effect it will produce. The Countess says: "There are emotions stronger than we are" (T II, 75), implying that the Marquise cannot stomach the truth, i.e., accept the fact the Chevalier is now the suitor of the Countess. But she is wrong; she has found her match in the Marquise. Eventually it will be she, the Countess, who is overcome by "emotions stronger than we": At the end of the play, she will faint and thus be forced to admit that her love for Dorante is still uppermost in her heart.

The Countess undergoes a gradual transformation. At the beginning, she jokes about infidelity (T II, 58-60); later she talks a very different language. When she discovers that she still loves Dorante, she curses her past vanity, tries to arrange a meeting with him, and undertakes to mend her ways (T II, 97f). She tells the Chevalier she does not love him (T II, 100). The trouble is that Dorante and the Marquise are adamant; they will not accept anything less than complete surrender from the Countess, and so it must come to the pretended marriage contract that convinces the Countess she is about to lose Dorante forever. She faints and thus shows her love (T II, 104); only then does Dorante respond and assure her of undying faithfulness. We can assume that the suffering he has inflicted on her will make their love that much more wonderful; it is the same pattern as in *Le Jeu de l'Amour* (only this time it is the girl who suffers).

There is cruelty also in the situation of Lisette and Arlequin, for they love each other and want to marry, but this seems impossible as long as their masters, Dorante and the Countess, are at odds. They seem to play not only with their own affections, but with those of their servants (Act II, Sc. 10). Arlequin and Lisette are heartbroken; they know what they want. Vanity does not force them to flirt or play the games of society (cf. *L'Île de la Raison*). They are much affected by the obstacles Dorante and the Countess impose on them.

The Chevalier and his valet, Frontin, provide amusement. The Chevalier is shiftless; he lacks character; he is, at best, the tool of the Countess' vanity, but not the object of her affection. We wonder how the Marquise can stand him. It is true that she merely promises to tell in six months whether she can marry him. He will have to reform, like the Petit-Maître Corrigé. Is he capable of such a feat?

Frontin is a buffoon. For a while he is used by the Countess to spy on Dorante and the Marquise. His observations are grotesque, consistently false. He reports:

Despair is something one can easily recognize. It is quite unlike the almost imperceptible and delicate emotions which escape detection. Those can deceive us, but despair is something definite, an emotion of consequence. Desperate people are agitated and jumpy. They are noisy. They make gestures, and here (looking at Dorante and the Marquise) there is none of that. (T II, 81)

He has no inkling that Dorante and the Marquise are embarked on a desperation course!

Frontin is funny also in his sardonic and useless pursuit of Lisette. When she is finally happy and able to marry Arlequin, Frontin gives her six months to be in his arms (T II, 105), the same length of time the Marquise gives the Chevalier, but for very different reasons. This is the last line of the play; it thereby takes on special significance. No one expects Lisette to become unfaithful to Arlequin, but the question remains, can love last? The "lucky stratagem" did rekindle it but for how long? It produced an overwhelming response. The intensity of emotion is emphasized by (alexandrine) verse in the prose dialogue:

COUNTESS: *Je défiais son coeur de me manquer jamais.* (T II, 97) (I dared his heart ever to be unfaithful.)

MARQUISE: *Rendez-vous à present; vous êtes aimé Dorante. (T II, 104) (Give in now, Dorante; you are loved.)*

Still, how many "lucky stratagems" will it take to make a marriage last? Must there be one every six months? Let us recall the line from the *Cabinet du Philosophe:* "Of all the ways to kill love, the easiest is to satisfy it" (OD, 338), and also the explanation that Valville who left Marianne for Varthon is not a monster for being unfaithful, but just an average lover in our times (M, 376). There is all too much uncertainty about the future for comfort. The happy ending may be an illusion! Frontin may yet be right!

VIII   Le Paysan Parvenu
(The Peasant who Gets Ahead in the World),
novel, in 5 parts: I-IV: 1734, V: 1735.

Jacob is Marianne's male counterpart. He advances toward success and wealth as she did, and not unlike Tom Jones later on. Like Marianne, he tells of his early days at a time when he has reached the age of fifty and is supporting a number of nephews (P, 8).

Jacob's biography presents an analagous picture but with significant differences. The novel is shorter and more unified in tone. The action is limited to the last two days of Jacob's first employment in Paris, and to eleven subsequent days during which he gets married and makes friends who can provide a life of ease for him. If Marianne is noble by birth and sentiment, Jacob, the son of a vintner from Champagne, starts from the bottom of the ladder, but he has good looks, he is adaptable, and rapidly learns the ways of refinement.

His father had sent him to Paris with a load of wine. The delivery led to his immediate employment and to the friendship, soon love, of one of the maids, Geneviève. While the girl is being corrupted and paid by their master, Jacob accepts some of her ill-gotten gains as presents; however, when the master tells him to marry her, he boldly refuses to become his front man; he pleads that he stems from a long line of virgins and cannot marry in sin (P, 29-30). "Poor people don't like to be cuckolds . . . . Geneviève may be distinguished enough to pay her compliments or bow to her; but I don't think that her distinction is sufficient for her to be the wife of a husband" (P, 28). In this passage, the word *honnêteté,* which we rendered by "distinction," concerns not only etiquette and politeness, but honor and the behavior of a gentleman; the pun involves all of the opposing meanings.

Jacob's refusal can be interpreted as an act of outraged virtue, and he proposes it that way, but he is tainted by his greed, and knows it. In any event, the sacrifice—he was to have been nicely provided for with Geneviève, had he complied—is followed by immediate dismissal, but also by greater fortune, for when he succors Mademoiselle Habert on the Pont-Neuf, she is delighted to adopt him. It is a parallel situation to Marianne's refusal to stay with Climal and subsequently meeting Madame de Miran.

The tone of the *Paysan Parvenu* is quite different from that of the other novel. Jacob goes much further in admitting his devious motives. He explains that he came to the rescue of Mademoiselle Habert not just out of sympathy, but because she is so well preserved. Marianne's frame of mind is consistently that of the masters in the plays; Jacob does not hide his peasant origins. When he arrives at the home of Mademoiselle Habert, he revels in the food and drink served by the maid, Catherine (P, 47-52). He is just like Arlequin in *La Double Inconstance,* invited by Flaminia to eat and drink, and forget Silvia.

Mademoiselle Habert loves Jacob. She is willing to give up the long association with her sister, their life devoted to piety and obedience to a confessor. She will marry Jacob and transform him into the facsimile of a nobleman, "Monsieur de la Vallée." She shows herself all the more passionate for having spent fifty years in a life of devotion: "What a pleasure to frustrate the devil and satisfy oneself, without sin, as readily as the sinners" (P, 183). Marianne would never have used such language, though she was quite aware of sensuality. She willingly showed her ankel when decency would allow her to do so.

Jacob has no trouble acting his new part. He rises naturally in society, like Silvia in *La Double Inconstance.* Soon after he receives the accoutrements of nobility, including a sword, he bravely intervenes in a street fight and saves the life of Count d'Orval who was quite unknown to him. It is a gratuitous act, but also the foundation of future influence and status, for Jacob has found an important and useful friend.

The same is true when he nobly declines the offer of a position from Monsieur de Fécour, because accepting it would have deprived a poor invalid of his livelihood. His renunciation so impresses a wealthy business man, Monsieur Bonno, that he too is ready to aid Jacob's career. The emerging gentleman in Jacob is what separates him from his picaresque ancestors like Gil Blas. Jacob grows into Monsieur de la Vallée; no *pícaro* would have been capable of that.

Furthermore, Jacob will prosper because he attracts the aid and devotion of female sponsors. It is true that the two ladies, beside Mademoiselle Habert, whom he befriends in the novel will not be mainstays for his future, but they indicate a pattern. First, there is Madame de Ferval. She is a hypocrite; her pious airs are enticing (P, 245). She helps him from prison where he was held because he was confused with a young assassin, a passionate young man who had wanted to kill his rival but slew the girl he loved. After extricating Jacob from this difficulty, Madame de Ferval uses him as her secretary and makes intimate advances. She pays his coach fare to visit her in her suburban retreat where she meets her lovers without compromising her religious front. Unlike Marianne, Jacob accepts such an invitation, but it turns out to be a frustrating experience. Another suitor interrupts and brings the "misery" of her existence much into evidence (P, 227).

The second lady is Madame de Fécour, who had sent Jacob to Versailles to solicit the protection of her brother. She is "more libertine than tender" (P, 180), and endowed with a tremendous bosom. Before long she becomes repulsive to Jacob; their flirtation is even more short-lived than the last. The two brief liaisons are exploited for comic effect when Jacob sets out to tell his wife all about his success just as she urges him to hurry to bed (P, 189).

Fewer "reflections" intervene in the *Paysan* than in *La Vie de Marianne*, but there is enough commentary on morals to justify a sizeable index in the 1748 edition, reproduced by Deloffre (P, 435f). It lists topics like God, the devil, education, women, love, the classes of society. Another difference between the two novels: There are fewer speeches in the *Paysan;* nonetheless, Jacob, like Marianne, can wax eloquent. He defends his marriage plans against the machinations of the older Mademoiselle Habert, the confessor, and relatives. Like Marianne before the Minister, Jacob pleads his case before the President. He triumphs as she had, but in a different style. Instead of her noble renunciation, he chooses to attack the enemy. He claims that he is the social equal of the Habert sisters, whose grandparents were farmers like his parents. Could one intervening generation of shopkeepers constitute a significant distinction? (P, 130).

Jacob picks and chooses his arguments cleverly. He completely glosses over the age difference of thirty years. In the *Cabinet du Philosophe,* a lady only five years older than the man she loved sees her plans distintegrate (OD, 423). A courtesy book of the time explains:

If, in her madness, an old woman marries her young beau, she sacrifices her honor, her mind, and her peace to her love affair. I know that such marriages fall within the limits of legality, but I, personally, shall always look upon them as legalized crimes.[4]

Jacob wins out in spite of such impressions! He is most persuasive—like Marivaux who was five years younger than his wife.

Three plays are related to the *Paysan Parvenu.* Jacob's rejection of Geneviève reappears in *Le Chemin de la Fortune* (1734), where Verdure refuses to marry Lisette who sleeps with her master: She is "a widow with a husband still alive," whereupon Fortune becomes very impatient with him (*Cabinet du Philosophe,* OD, 367). Jacob facing the Habert sisters, one wishing to marry him, the other trying to undo these plans, recalls Ergaste in *La Méprise* (1734), with one comic difference: Ergaste, who is attracted by Hortense and repulsed by Clarice, cannot tell them apart since they wear identical disguises.

The third related play, *La Commère* (1741) lifts an entire episode from the *Paysan,* the first attempt of Mademoiselle Habert and Jacob to be married. In the novel it was foiled by Madame d'Alain, not only because she is so talkative and broadcasts the plans, but because she asks the confessor of the Habert sisters to perform the ceremony. This priest, who sees his power threatened, flatly refuses. In the novel, a second attempt succeeds. *La Commère* modifies all this. A nephew is introduced who uncovers all. The play emphasizes the "gossip" of Madame d'Alain. The marriage plans are ruined for good.

Like *Marianne, Le Paysan Parvenu* remains incomplete. It is clear that Monsieur de la Vallée's good fortune is imminent. What remains to be told is obvious.[5]

IX   Le Cabinet du Philosophe
(The Philosopher's Study),
journal in 11 issues, 1734.

We have referred a number of times to the "leaflets" of this periodical, because it contains some of Marivaux' most explicit statements on essential issues closely related to the novels and plays published around this time. We shall discuss first two longer segments included in the *Cabinet, Le Chemin de la liberté,* an allegorical play, and the philosophical tale entitled *Le Voyageur dans le Nouveau Monde, ou Le Monde Vrai.* After that we shall turn to the short "reflections," purposely interspersed so as to provide variety for the reader, and to sneak in serious matter without losing the mundane public.

In *Le Chemin de la Fortune (The Way to Fortune)*, goddess Fortune is waiting for those willing to jump over a moat to reach her, an easy task which merely requires abandoning virtue and morals. Tombs can be seen all around with such inscriptions as: "Here lies the innocence of a young girl; Here lies hard work needed to earn a living" (OD, 356). Scruple manages to dissuade Greenface ("Verdure"), an inexperienced youth, from jumping *(ibid.)*, but not Brash ("Rondelet"), an unscrupulous profiteer (OD, 367-68). Hermidas, a dull author, puts Fortune to sleep with his orations and is therefore barred from access; he will be able to attain wealth only by malice, like most critics; Marivaux is no more charitable toward them now than ever before! (OD, 370). Clarice, who dreams of a tender husband because she is sick of her sensuous lovers, just nauseates Fortune; how is a girl like Clarice to become wealthy? (OD, 361). Lucidor is a better prospect; he hates to see his little virtues buried in this countryside, but the priest of the goddess convinces him that he can easily rid him of such scruples (OD, 371). Ultimately these characters represent aspects of Marianne and Jacob on their way to wealth; they are commentaries on the novels. So conceived, the allegory finds ample illustration in concrete situations, and once again shows the realism of Marivaux in a setting of fantasy.

Le Monde Vrai (The Traveller to a New World, or the World of Truth) is a short novel (OD, 389-419, 428-37). It takes the Chevalier to an unknown country which, to his surprise, is just like the Paris he knows, except that everyone states his opinions with unabashed frankness. His guide explains that the trip will teach him to know man (OD, 418-19). *Le Diable Boiteux (The Limping Devil)* by Lesage is similar in intent, though less ambitious in analyzing pretense and true motives. Marivaux proposes neither utopia nor reform, for the admission of the truth does not change anyone's action.

Folville is to marry Mademoiselle Dinval. Her making up to the Chevalier shows her to be a flirt who will be unfaithful to her husband. Folville knows it well, but explains that, since he cannot admit this to himself, he will not ask the Chevalier to leave her (OD, 410).

A man, whom the Chevalier has always considered to be his close friend, mails him the announcement of his uncle's illness, but so late that the Chevalier almost misses out on a large inheritance. He manages to see his uncle before he dies and does not lose out on the money as his "friend" had hoped. At that point the father who had refused to let his daughter marry the Chevalier, shamelessly writes: "Now that you are so wealthy, I hope you are still anxious to marry my daughter" (OD, 434). The Chevalier declines the compliment, but what if he had fallen for the hypocrisy of the real Paris?

Marivaux is not given to despair: "Eternity is not all deceit" (OD, 390). The idea consoles him. Nonetheless, the impact of deceit would be overwhelming, were it not for the presence of the guide who carries on him a book entitled, *The Story of the Human Heart* (OD, 395). The episodes serve as its illustrations. Man may be utterly self-centered, but the Chevalier does not lose his faith in humanity.

The shorter reflections contained in the *Cabinet du Philosophe* read like marginal comments that did not find their place in *Marianne* or the *Paysan;* they are equally critical but accept man such as he is; after all, the study of man remains the object and justification of all of Marivaux' writing.

One group of these reflections concerns the everpresent theme of love. "If they thought about it, women would blush at the consideration and respect we have for them" (OD, 355). Good manners are the camouflage imposed by polite society: "Tell a woman, 'I desire you greatly, please grant me your favors,' and she will reject your brutishness, but tell her, 'I love you, you have a thousand charms,' and she will listen and be pleased, though you have said the same thing; you have used the language of a gentleman" (OD, 337). Thus, coquettes and their male equivalent, the gallant man, are to be considered as normal human beings (cf. M, 376). After all, "the immodesty of the prettiest girl appeals the most" (M, 374) and eternal faithfulness is found only in utopia, in outdated novels (OD, 375). Such is not the reality of love. It can be grotesque, as when a woman marries a younger man (OD, 421-23). Love is perverted by faults of character: A girl who rudely upbraids her maid was wisely abandoned by her fiancé, for the person she later married just about died from the grief she inflicted on him (OD, 427-28). What are we to say, then, of Tervire, in the last scene of *La Vie de Marianne?* Whom will she be able to love with her spirit of righteous indignation? The convent must be her solution. Once again, *Cabinet du Philosophe* illuminates the novel.

Injustice is recognized in the double standard applied to men and women. A woman's adultery is sternly punished, while an unfaithful husband is not restrained and may even be admired (OD, 376). The poor are often the victims of our institutions. The death penalty is imposed on men trying to end their poverty. Is the punishment not more cruel than the crime it is to remedy? As Marivaux well knows, poverty brings not just inconvenience, but makes one feel inferior and ashamed (OD, 362). Few were the men, like Helvétius, from whom he felt he could accept money without lowering himself. The poverty of Marianne and Tervire are good illustrations to the point.

Another reflection condemns those who covet wealth, also the vainglorious, obnoxious, and overly ambitious (OD, 437). What then of Marianne and Jacob? Is their progress not unscrupulous, even though their selfless actions seem attractive, as they are anxious to point out? Their ambivalence is human, but their desire to advance is all too strong. Marivaux' reflections are most humorous when applied to the situations of his novels and plays.

One of the important sections of *Le Cabinet du Philosophe* concerns style. Marivaux reacts to his critics, especially to their attack on the second part of *Marianne* where Madame Dutour hurls insults at the coachman. More urgently than in 1719, he stresses the interdependence of form (*"style"*) and ideas. This, he says, is what critics misunderstand when they accuse him of excessive "finesse," when they call him overrefined, desirous merely to appear brilliant (OD, 345). He cites Montaigne, Pascal, La Rochefoucauld, and La Bruyère in his defense and adds that, were they still alive, the critics would condemn them just as bitterly for being precious (OD, 376-78). What hurts most is that critics join ridicule to insult; how can their personal attacks be productive? (OD, 388-89) Marivaux never replied in kind; he refused to write a pamphlet against Voltaire's *Lettres Philosophiques*.

The abbé du Bos had stated that "words are the figures of our ideas" (*Réflexions* I, Sec. 33-34). Marivaux goes further by seeking appropriate "signs" for particular ideas (OD, 380f, 383f); he is conscious of the uniqueness of each situation and will use new words to describe it if need be; this is what shocked the purists, but he is always clear. His objective is neither wit *(esprit)* nor unusual effects, but insight *(pénétration),* the exact expression of what is on his mind. He is fascinated with language and molds it to his use; he even develops elements of linguistic analysis when he distinguishes words that denote concepts form those that "link" them, e.g., articles (OD, 383-84).

Not unrelated to matters of style are his comments on the *Je ne sais quoi,* the undefinable charm of the unsuspected. In the *Entretiens d'Eugène et d'Ariste,* Bouhours considered the term to include poetic embellishments; Marivaux rejects the figures of rhetoric. He welcomes the *Je ne sais quoi* as the antithesis of ostentatious harmony. To him it represents the beauty of a discreet English garden, apparently unplanned, for he dislikes the pompous geometry of its French equivalent (OD, 346-51). Surprise, newness, the unsuspected, are to him ends in themselves. This explains the whimsical structure of his periodicals or of his plays. At times they end unexpectedly with the solution everyone expected.

The commentary on religion in the *Cabinet* is notable. *L'Ile de la Raison* had shown the Philosophe incapable of reform and understood reason as the realization of one's faults, an attitude of humility rather than assertiveness. In this spirit he now rejects atheists and their rationalistic arguments which preclude alternatives (OD, 426) and deists who set themselves up as their own judges (OD, 419). For all this, he does not prefer the show of orthodoxy; priests are often credulous or vainglorious; hypocrites and deluded practitioners of religion abound in *Marianne* and the *Paysan*.

He does, however, honor religious faith. He compares our health, which requires that we give up certain pleasures, and the prince who rightfully demands that we sacrifice part of our freedom to the State, with religion that demands that we sacrifice part of our reason (OD, 341-42), or rather, conceive reason so as to be reconcilable with religion, as it is in *L'Ile de la Raison*. Here Marivaux comes close to Rousseau's "reason of the heart." "In religion, reason only for man's heart," he advises, "all the rest is mystery" (OD, 352-53). Elsewhere he says that religion is half sacrifice of self, half mystery, the mystery of faith that cannot be questioned (OD, 341-42). Without belittling reason, Marivaux sets limits for it. He tells us that those who believe in God communicate their faith like birds in the air. He admits that this phenomenon will seem strange to nonbelievers (OD, 353).

When he explains that crime cannot be wiped out by punishment but should be constrained by the fear of God (OD, 364), he appears as a pragmatist like Voltaire and we must add that the passages mocking false devotion and religious hypocrisy *(les dévots)* far outnumber those that define the mystery of faith. Still, these also are sincere. Marivaux significantly echoes the religious rationalism of Malebranche. References to him are frequent in the *Cabinet du Philosophe* (OD, footnotes IV 52, 53, 60, 69, 88, 89, 135, 170, and corresponding passages in the text).

Marivaux' evolution can be characterized by the following comparison: In his first novel he includes a utopia. In the *Télémaque Travesti* he rejects it as not belonging to our world. In the *Cabinet* he adopts a more clearly theological position which involves terms like divine order *(ordre)*, God, eternity, mysteries, and chains that mark man's impotence (OD, 353, 355). He asserts that only the true believer is entirely free (*superbe,* OD, 364). This vocabulary reflects his positive attitude toward religion. It does not show reserved judgment or agnosticism. In brief reflections, cautiously, and bit by bit, Marivaux takes his stand on the side of religion, even while he remains the sharp critic of many religious practices and an author intent on amusing his public rather than lecturing to his reader.

X   La Méprise
(A Case of Mistaken Identity),
comedy in one act, T. I., 1734.

If we will grant that two sisters, Cydalise and the younger Hortense, can be indistinguishable in their masquerade costumes (in Lyon, where such parties are supposed to be common) and that Ergaste can be in love with Cydalise without being able to tell her apart from the jealous and negative Hortense, then *La Méprise* is a delightful, hilarious, brief play. In his confusion, Ergaste makes a passionate declaration of love to Hortense. She is startled and becomes furious when she sees him addressing Cydalise the same way. Hortense comes close to slapping Frontin because he brings her a love letter from Ergaste obviously intended for Cydalise. She refuses to read it. Meanwhile Arlequin's high spirits add comedy.

The play continues a long tradition, the theme of two sisters confused. Dancourt, who stands closest to Marivaux in his use of natural, quick dialogue, provides the immediate source, *Les Fêtes Nocturnes du Cours* (T II, 3-4, 109-10), but the rivalry of Lucile and Phénice in *Les Serments Indiscrets* is equally significant as a parallel.

XI   Le Petit-Maître Corrigé
(The Fop Reformed),
comedy in 3 acts, T. F., 1734.

Written in 1732-33, the *Petit-Maître Corrigé* was not performed until the year following, owing to the controversy concerning *Les Serments Indiscrets.* To overcome hostility and impress the more difficult public of the Comédie Française, Marivaux composed a play which combines comedy with the critique of a particular social type, the "*petit-maître*"; Dancourt had defined such fops as "playful gentlemen who talk a lot and say little, sigh tenderly but are lovers for purposes of conversation only, grand in their manners but without resources, generous in promises and declarations of friendship, inventors of fashions and airs" (cited T II, 855, n. 32). One contemporary objects to their "habit of ridiculing sentiment" (cited T II, 148); Marivaux' hero, Rosimond, is as guilty of this as the pedants portrayed in earlier plays, those unaware of the feelings and power of love: Hortensius in the second *Surprise,* Hermocrate and Léontine in *Le Triomphe de l'Amour,* and others. However, Rosimond also has meritorious qualities. He can be reformed like the shipwrecked Europeans in *L'Île de la Râison.* Rosimond becomes "reasonable." Musset used this plot in *Il ne Faut Jurer de Rien,* just as he had adapted *Les Serments Indiscrets* in *On ne Badine pas avec L'Amour;* Musset adroitly picked two plays which Marivaux had not been able to make as dramatically successful as their subject deserved.

For there is much of interest. Rosimond is returning to the country from Paris. Like the "précieuses ridicules," he believes that he has mastered Parisian manners. He takes on the airs of a man of the world and treats Hortense, destined by parental consent to become his wife, with such flippancy that he almost destroys their love. He acts like a harmless Don Juan, disgracefully overconfident, and tries to take after Dorante, a true Parisian fop, his rival for the affections of Hortense. Frontin does his best to imitate Rosimond. They have no idea how ridiculous they are until Marton tells Frontin that everyone is laughing at him and his master. As in *L'Île de la Raison,* the servant is first to change; then Rosimond is gradually transformed into his true, likable self. Even so he remains awkward, a straight man who recites obvious truths without being able to convince Hortense that he loves her, or Dorimène, who wants him for a husband, that he will never marry her. He is a pathetic figure. To his despair, Hortense will even intercede with Rosimond's mother, the Marquise, to obtain approval for his marriage with Dorimène.

Rosimond faces an impasse. All he can do is swallow his pride and fall on his knees; he bursts forth that his love for Hortense is eternal! No, he will never have Dorimène! Once Rosimond mocked sentiment, now he is overpowered by it. Hortense, touched by his sincerity, agrees to become his wife.

Rosimond's surrender is much like that of the Countess at the end of *L'Heureux Stratagème,* only here the man capitulates! There are other parallels. In neither play are we sure that the second couple will marry: The Chevalier is much like Dorante, more noted for his airs and promises than for action (marriage) and sentiment. It is as if Marivaux had constructed the two plays like variations on a theme, which involves character analysis, for this element takes precedence over social commentary concerning the role or qualities of the *petit-maître* (fop).

Even with its weaknesses, the play did not deserve the resounding failure that was its fate. A cabal was at work. It could come from two directions, or from both combined. Crébillon Fils had mocked Marivaux in a scene of *Tanzaï et Néadarné* where Marivaux appears as a mole, called Moustache, and utters precious phrases he does not understand. Marivaux had countered the attack by having an old army officer, a straightforward, honest man, tell a young author that the abuse of libertine situations for popular success is undeserving of him, unworthy of a creative mind. This scene in the *Paysan Parvenu* (P, 199-201) provoked Matucci's comment that this novel was written as a model for Crébillon to follow.[6] Crébillon did not take the correction kindly; not only was *Tanzaï* condemned as too licentious, but he was jailed. His friends may well have organized the cabal, noise so loud that one could not hear the actors at the first performance of the *Petit-Maître*.

Besides Crébillon, there was Voltaire, attacked for his *Lettres Philosophiques*, fearful that Marivaux would launch a pamphlet against him (*Correspondence*, Besterman ed., 968) and in a better position to launch a cabal than Crébillon in jail. Later we shall find Voltaire competing unsuccessfully with Marivaux for a seat in the French Academy (1742) and composing *Nanine, ou le Préjugé Vaincu* (1749) to outdo Marivaux' *Préjugé Vaincu* (1746). We have cited his unfavorable comment on *Les Serments* (cf. Besterman, 478). We find a continuing rivalry, which affected Marivaux' long-standing effort to succeed on the major Parisian stage; once again he had been foiled (cf. T II, 157f).

XII   La Mère Confidente
(The Mother as a Confidante),
comedy in 3 acts, T. I., 1735.

In a remarkable transformation of *L'Ecole des Mères,* Marivaux produced one of the first and perhaps the best sentimental comedy, or bourgeois drama of his day. It appeared before *Le Préjugé Vaincu* by Nivelle de la Chaussée who has generally been credited with creating the new genre. Marivaux' part was at least equally important.

Finding her daughter in love with the young and penniless Dorante, Madame Argante wants to arrange a better marriage for her. Her choice is Ergaste, thirty-five years old, wealthy, but also, as Angélique knows all too well, cold, taciturn, and moody (T II, 244). It is not known until later that Ergaste is the uncle of Dorante. Thus the silly and sensuous old man, the sixty-year-old father in *L'Ecole des Mères*, has been replaced by a much more likely and formidable rival for the young man, somber but honorable, rich, not too old. The role of the mother is also changed, for the new Madame Argante wants to be Angélique's confidante. Initially she wants to dissuade Angélique, but when she finds this impossible, she agrees to meet Dorante, disguised as a disinterested aunt, so as not to arouse his antagonism. She convinces the couple not to elope and ruin their future life and reputation, but in her turn she is touched by Dorante's honest repentance: He considers himself unworthy of her, since it was he who had suggested elopement. Madame Argante is so moved by his noble renunciation that she is willing to accept him as a son-in-law (T II, 278).

The paradox is characteristic of Marivaux. In spite of his poverty, Dorante is accorded Angélique for his willingness to give her up. Only later does he receive a handsome dowry from Ergaste, who decided that he must not marry if he is not loved. Just as in the novels, virtue is rewarded all too well. Virtue attracts, but let us ask: What has the nobly repentant Dorante given up? An abduction! Is it virtuous to forego a crime? Is guilt an asset because one can be so appealingly sorry for it? *Les Fausses Confidences* illustrates the quandary.

Madame Argante is also an ambivalent character. In a way she resembles Madame de Miran in *La Vie de Marianne*. the noble creation inspired by Madame de Lambert. Madame Argante is truly the confidante of Angélique. On the other hand, she may be adopting this role to govern her daughter more easily. Her disguise as an "objective" observer is hilarious: Is the authority of a mother best exercised with a mask? In the *Jeu*, the shortest road to the truth is the mask! Can Madame Argante be considered a selfless advisor when she is not disguised? Is she accepting Dorante as a son-in-law only because he seems so appealingly obedient and does not elope?

Madame Argante has her difficult moments. She fires the faithful Lisette because she espouses the young people's cause; Madame Argante even insists that the young couple, when married, fire her also (T II, 279). We can assume that they will not heed such advice but it proves that this kind mother can be spiteful and headstrong!

Of course, the opposite interpretation is equally plausible. Madame Argante is a good mother; she does her best to combat her authoritarian disposition and her temper; she is willing to let her daughter marry Dorante even without money, most unlike the parents in Molière who agree to the young man's marriage only after they inherit a fortune.

Madame Argante does make a notable effort to stay in touch with the young people.

How then are we to judge her? As a human being, with varied qualities. It is interesting to note how different critical evaluations have been, presenting her as the ideal of the understanding mother, or then again as an authoritarian parent who resorts to vile tricks.

All this shows that Marivaux maintains the spirit of comedy even when he deals with serious problems affecting sentiment. The hilarious role of Lubin is further proof. When Dorante explains that making the acquaintance of Angélique was mere accident and that, if he bowed to salute her, he was only obeying the requirements of polite society, Lubin replies: "And does your bow express itself in words?" One critic of 1735 was outraged that the wittiest passages were put into the mouth of a peasant (T II, 226, 239).

It has often been claimed that Marivaux deals only with internal obstacles, since his approach is "psychological," but *Le Petit-Maître Corrigé* deals with social conventions and modes of hehavior, *La Mère Confidente* with the conflict between generations and financial requirements for marriage; the latter theme becomes central in the next play, *Le Legs*. Rank and social status were the issue in *La Double Inconstance* and *Le Prince Travesti,* also in the island plays and in *Le Jeu de l'Amour,* where the obstacle of rank, even though imagined, has to be overcome by Dorante. In the novels this is equally true. Marianne and Jacob rise in society; Jacob goes to jail, becomes wealthy because he engages in a street fight: his good looks aid him everywhere. Marianne lets Valville look at her ankle and rouses his passion. In *La Mère Confidente* Dorante meets Angélique because she has lost her hat. Marivaux presents his characters in a very'real context, the fantasy of the setting notwithstanding. *La Mère Confidente* was such a success because it illustrated the family relationship in a new light, with human affection and sympathy.

XIII   Le Legs
(The Inheritance),
comedy in 1 act, T. F., 1736.

This one-act play for the Comédie Française seems to parody *Les Serments Indiscrets* and its frustrating delays. Once again the situation is clear from the beginning. The Marquis wants to marry the Countess, Hortense and the Chevalier also plan to marry. There is an obstacle, money, but the Marquis is so wealthy that the financial advantage he would have in marrying Hortense matters little to him. What holds up everything is his timidity; he does not dare tell the Countess he loves her.

The matter of finance is spelled out in great detail. The Marquis had inherited 600,000 francs ($1,200,000; 400,000 francs in the first stage version). He must leave one-third of this sum to Hortense, should he refuse to marry her, but he needs to leave her nothing if she refuses to marry him. The sum represents a veritable fortune to the poverty-stricken Chevalier and to Hortense who will not forfeit her claim. She puts it rather grossly to the Chevalier: "You are not wealthy enough to marry me without the 200,000 francs, and I intend to bring them to you as a dowry" (T II, 304).

This reduces the Chevalier to a pathetic position. He must pretend to believe that the Marquis will marry Hortense (Sc. 12); he must bear insults as when the Countess tells him: "What sordid avarice! What heart without feeling! And people like you say that they are in love! What dirty love! You may leave, I have nothing to add!" (T II, 329). All this even though the Chevalier is sincere in his love; to please Hortense he may not defend himself! Let us ask: Who is speaking to him in these terms? The same Countess who advises the Marquis not to forego any part of his recent inheritance, the Countess who is wealthy enough to have 1000 francs in her home and is ready to lend them to the Marquis, carries on a bitter lawsuit over an equivalent amount elsewhere. The Countess is a brusque woman; she needs a meek and timid husband like the Marquis. She would have him, if only he would declare himself . . . .

Somehow the Marquis has convinced himself that the Countess does not love him. Lisette is in part responsible. Lisette wants to prevent the match to safeguard her influence and income. Her counterpart, Lépine, valet of the Marquis, is different however. He wagers that he will marry Lisette when their masters marry and does all he can to bring them together. Lépine offers his services to Hortense and accepts her money, but when it comes to fetching a notary to marry her to the Marquis—she keeps pursuing him so no one can say it was she who turned down this match—Lépine claims to be busy, then ill, even "dead" as he puts it, all so the Marquis, his master, will keep his freedom and be united to the Countess he loves. Lépine warns the Countess of Lisette's schemes: "Can one keep an ant from crawling?" Lépine asks; "her lowly condition is responsible for her low ideas" (T

II, 332). Eventually Lisette will accept that the Countess marry the Marquis and Lépine has his way; he becomes Lisette's husband; throughout, he pulls the strings. As a servant-mastermind he will soon be followed by Dubois in *Les Fausses Confidences,* a play which also has some of the financial detail of *Le Legs.*

In early plays the servants married when their masters did; the pair in *Les Serments Indiscrets* rebel against their masters' plans until the power of money forces them to give in. Lépine and Lisette create a new situation: They work against each other for some time, though they could be happy together, somewhat like the Marquis who almost prevents the match he desires because he cannot believe he is loved. When, finally, his true feeling breaks through with all its awkwardness—the Marquis is less melodramatic than Rosimond, the Petit-Maître, and more touching—he has confessed that he would love the Countess, were it not for her aversion.

COUNTESS: You say you love me, don't you, and I believe you, but tell me, how would you want me to respond?
MARQUIS: What I would want? Is that so hard to guess? Besides, you know! (T II, 336)

But still he won't say the word; only when she threatens to leave does he get his courage together:

MARQUIS: Well, lady, I love you. What do you think of that? . . . Again, what do you think?
COUNTESS: Oh, what I think? That I like the idea, and again, that I like it, because, if I did not admit that I like it, we would never be done. (T II, 337)

And so, Hortense and the Chevalier can get their 200,000 francs; they are able to marry in the style of the society to which they belong. The Marquis is only too happy to sacrifice this amount to marry the Countess.

An interesting sidelight is provided by Fontenelle's play, *Le Testament,* Marivaux' principal source. There is an analogous plot with a different ending, for Philonoé (Hortense) is so touched by the willingness of the philosopher Eudamidas (the Marquis) to let some of his inheritance endow another marriage, that she marries him after all. Marivaux' characters marry for love, not out of admiration; his disinterested philosophers, like Ergaste in *La Mère Confidente,* are likely to remain bachelors, even when they are not pedants like Hortensius in the second *Surprise*. Marivaux knows the role of love and emotion far better than Fontenelle.

Le Legs admirably combines the external obstacle, the money problem, with the study of motivation, the characterizations of the timid Marquis, the forward Countess, Hortense the realist, the humiliated Chevalier, and Lépine, bright, funny, and always in control. The play has been one of the long-standing successes on the stage, except when it was first produced; in 1736 the cabal directed against Marivaux' *Petit-Maître* was still entrenched at the Comédie Française; even the fact that the play was presented anonymously did not protect it.

XIV   Les Fausses Confidences
(False Confessions),
comedy in 3 acts, T. I., 1737.

We now turn to Marivaux' last longer play, one rightfully considered to be his masterpiece, along with *Le Jeu de l'Amour*. Its greatness lies in the original combination of sentiment and humor in a realistic setting. The title refers to the schemes of Dubois, invented so that his master can marry Araminte. As a young widow, her enviable situation is one of independence and wealth. She is free to marry as she wishes and need not heed her mother, Madame Argante, who vehemently favors Count Dorimont because such a match would add the rank of nobility to the family fortune. Count Dorimont, in turn, is interested, for besides wealth, the marriage can assure him of a large tract of land to which Araminte has a better claim than he.

Dorante is introduced into her household by her attorney, his uncle, Monsieur Remy, Dorante is to be Araminte's business manager, much to the displeasure of Count Dorimont, who wants to introduce his front man into this position, and of Madame Argante who knows that Dorante will tell her that her claims to the land are good; he will be an obstacle to Araminte's union with the Count. As Madame Argante puts it, Araminte "should be deceived in her own best interest" (T II, 369). How else can she become a Countess?

Dorante prides himself on being honest and tender in his love for Araminte, but ambition is lurking in the background, and he accepts Dubois' devious plans to make the girl fall in love with him. First Dubois warns Araminte that Dorante is crazy, for love of her; not a man to retain as her manager. As expected, this has the opposite effect and assures Dorante of the position; it also dissociates Dubois from Dorante in her mind. Then Dubois invents a number of proofs of Dorante's passion. He arranges for Araminte's portrait, supposedly painted by Dorante, to fall into her hands. Later he plants a letter in which Dorante asks a friend to accompany him to America since his love is so desperate. Why does Dubois do all this? Surely he is attached to Dorante whom he has served before working for Araminte; he wants to assure Dorante's happiness, but he also wants to prove his skill in influencing those about him; ambivalence is everpresent.

Marton, a girl of excellent family reduced by financial need to be Araminte's lady-in-waiting, plays a rather pathetic role in all this. Monsieur Remy wants his nephew to marry her. Marton falls in love with Dorante; besides, Count Dorimont promises her a considerable bribe if he can marry Araminte. Dorante is shocked (T II, 370), but who is he to show indignation? Then Monsieur Remy changes his mind; he wants Dorante to marry one of his clients, a lady of thirty-five whose income is considerable and guaranteed (T II, 380). When Dorante resists, Marton is sure he does so for her sake; she also believes that the portrait painted by Dorante is of her! How disillusioned she will be when the likeness turns out to be that of Araminte.

Unwittingly, Marton helps to bring Araminte closer to Dorante. Marton seizes Dorante's letter (about emigrating to America) from Arlequin and delivers it to Count Dorimont, who reads it to the assembled company as Dubois had planned. All Marton has left is her friendship for her rival, Araminte; the relationship resembles that of Hortense and the Princess in *Le Prince Travesti;* Marton is an unfortunate counterpart of Hortense, never lucky, never successful. She consoles herself with Araminte. Friendship is all she can hope for, love is denied. Marton's role is closest to the luckless Clorine in *Les Effets Surprenants.*

Dubois' plans do work. Araminte is furious that Dorante wrote the letter expressing his love for her, for it has become common knowledge; still, she does not want him to leave; she is in love with him. Sure of his victory, Dorante confesses that all, so far, was pretense except his passion for her, which is infinite (T II, 409, 415-16). His sincerity makes him even more appealing. She will marry him because she has learned about his tricks from him and no one else.

Such ambiguous honesty is typical of Marivaux. Let us recall *La Mère Confidente* and Dorante's repentance for wanting to elope with Angélique, also the episodes where Marianne and Jacob give up wealth for the sake of virtue and are rewarded with greater fortune, or a permission to marry beyond their state. Each instance is different and firmly anchored in the concrete circumstances of a particular situation. In *Les Fausses Confidences* there are negotiations concerning land and financial management, the fake portrait, and the deceitful letter, to add substance to sentiment.

The ending of the play preserves its realistic tone. The Count accepts his fate; Araminte will not press her claims. The victory of love is accompanied by a kind of peace treaty where Araminte's generosity is as evident as in her willingness to marry Dorante; he is not rich but with her fortune, she can afford it!

This solution leaves Madame Argante frustrated and furious. She shouts to Araminte: "Dorante may be your husband if you like, he will never be my son-in-law!" Whereupon Dubois: "My, my, such glorious success weighs on my shoulders; I might call the girl my daughter-in-law!" (T II, 417) as if he were to replace Madame Argante in Araminte's family circle.

The range of characterization is notable in this play. From Madame Argante, the unpleasant and absurd social climber, to the tender love of the young couple—and their hardheaded planning—with Dubois as Dorante's scheming alter ego, then again to the upright but heavy-handed Monsieur Remy, a typical bourgeois concerned with profits, and to Count Dorimont, the improverished and financially interested nobleman pursuing dubious claims! Dubois is remarkable among Marivaux' servants, a new type who pulls the strings and goes far beyond Arlequin in *La Double Inconstance* (who protests against the infringements on his rights and love on the part of the Prince) and Trivelin in *La Fausse Suivante* (who would take advantage of having discovered that the Chevalier is Silvia in disguise), also the servants in the island plays who temporarily dominate their masters, and Lépine in *Le Legs,* whose special talents we have noted. There will be Merlin, in *Les Acteurs de Bonne Foi,* to continue in Dubois' footsteps, and later Figaro, the great creation of Beaumarchais.

The fact that the plot derives from Lope's *Perro del hortolano (Dog in the Manger)* and its numerous adaptations (one by Riccoboni) detracts nothing from the original portrayals of this play. Its spirit is original, its structure perfectly balanced. It combines biting analysis of motives with excellent humor. It remains a masterpiece.

Its influence on Rousseau's *New Heloïse* is a special tribute to Marivaux. Marton's friendship for Araminte is like Claire's for Julie. Araminte's argument for keeping Dorante as her manager, that seeing her might cure him of his passion, is like Julie who invites Saint-Preux to be the tutor of her children for the same reason. Dorante speaks of emigrating to America; Saint-Preux embarks for there. Marivaux and Rousseau were acquainted. Marivaux corrected Rousseau's *Narcisse.* The analogies are suggestive of other parallels.[7]

XV   La Joie Imprévue
(Joy Unforeseen),
comedy in 1 act, T. I., 1738.

This "curtain raiser," written to accompany *Les Fausses Confidences,* is considered unimportant by some critics, but there is a striking display of wit and sentiment. There are two plots. The first describes the love of Damon for Constance. If Damon only delivered the letter his father, Orgon, has given him when he left for the city, they would already be planning a wedding, for the letter is addressed to the parents of Constance and expresses Orgon's hope to unite the children. This is unknown to the young people who fear their parents' plans on general principle. The outcome is even more expected than in *Le Dénouement Imprévu* where there was at least another contender, Dorante, with whom Mademoiselle Argante had a long-standing if meaningless flirtation. There is no obstacle beside Damon's distrust, the failure to carry out his father's instructions even though Pasquin is there to remind him (the servant is no longer Arlequin, for the actor of this role, Thomassin, is ill and will die the following year).

The second plot shows Damon as a gambler who has already lost half the money his father gave him to buy a position *(charge)* that would sustain him in the future; he is about to lose the other half. Here again, Pasquin, well-intentioned and faithful, cannot make Damon follow Orgon's advice; moral lectures are habitually ineffective in Marivaux! Fortunately, his partner, in his disguise at a costume ball, is not the Chevalier who has fleeced him before and is expected for a return engagement, but Orgon who has found out from Pasquin how precarious the position of his son has become. He turns out to be a most "reasonable" father. He wins the rest of his son's money; then he reveals his identity and, with a few words of advice about gambling, lets Damon keep the money.

There is wit, there is surprise even though the outcome is expected, the marriage of Damon and Constance; ineffectual moral advice is characteristic of Marivaux who believed that people learn mostly from experience, certainly not from lectures or well-meaning books. The transition, in the end, from Damon's despair at having ruined his future and rendered his marriage impossible, to the discovery that all is all right anyhow, provides once again a dramatic contrast between love and suffering. *La Joie Imprévue* is hilarious and effective and restates a number of the central themes of Marivaux.

XVI Les Sincères
(A Case of Sincerity), ·
comedy in 1 act, T. I., 1739.

The Marquise has invited three close friends to her château in the country: her Romanesque suitor, Dorante, her latest infatuation, the naïve and awkward Ergaste, and Araminte whom Ergaste used to court. Ergaste has brought his valet, Frontin, who dreams of the "incomparable Marton" whom Araminte has left in Paris.

The Marquise has tired of Dorante's eternal declarations of love which, she tells him, belong in dated novels of romance (T II, 483); she has taken Ergaste from Araminte and is fascinated by his unusual frankness. Frontin, who can have Marton only if their masters are reunited, therefore makes plans with Lisette, the maid of the Marquise, to break up her new love for Ergaste; in their droll manner, the two servants decide to quarrel among themselves to make sure of their success; if they undertake to fight, how could their masters stay together? It all sounds like a joke at the expense of stage conventions, but it seems to work. At the very end of the play we find Lisette refusing even a hug from Frontin, to celebrate their victory.

The movements of the two couples who have traded partners before the play begins, and trade back again as their affections crystallize, resemble those of a stylized ballet. They step in and out of each other's lives, surprised by the wiles of their own sensitivity. They are far more surprised than the audience that, at the end, the original alliances have been reconstituted (T II, 498). The fact that the spectator can say: "I told you so," flatters him; it is a key to the success of Marivaux' humor.

The title implies a good deal of irony, for as the Marquise and Ergaste set out to be truly sincere and tell each other what they think, they hurt each other's feelings badly. The straightforwardness of Alceste in the *Misanthrope* is on their minds, and so they forget to consider human needs. The Marquise vaingloriously describes the people she meets as fools and fops, but from Ergaste she expects only compliments (T II, 476-79). She cannot tolerate the same "sincerity" in return, the embarrassing comparisons he makes, for he calls Araminte more beautiful than she, even though he adds that she, the Marquise, is "far more pleasing" (T II, 486). Sarcastically she replies that he too is "pleasing" (T II, 489), quite unaware that Ergaste, who constantly deprecates his own talents, is eagerly awaiting compliments that will contradict his humiliating confessions. We feel how much the Marquise really needs Dorante who coddles her vanity and how Ergaste requires the affectionate understanding of Araminte. Ergaste's self-abasement is an illustration of La Rochefoucauld's maxim: "Declining praise shows the desire to be praised again."

Araminte realizes this. When Ergaste tells her in his despair: "I shall never seem appealing to anyone!" she answers that he is his own worst enemy and that he must be in love with her. Ergaste confesses this is true, but adds a phrase she could easily have taken to be an insult: "I believe it only because I am so foolish." She knows he is merely expressing his insecurity and plays along with him. She refuses to say whether she returns his love, but sends for the notary to draw up a marriage contract. "Shall I forgive you?" she asks him. "I don't deserve it," is his reply. "Quite so and I don't love you any more, but when the notary comes, we shall see further" (T II, 496-98). And so their marriage is decided and that of the Marquise with Dorante as well. The notary can do double duty.

Les Sincères is a delightful commentary on the illusions and the surprises of the heart. Sincerity is not on trial, for the ill-conceived obsession of the Marquise to criticize others, and of Ergaste to deprecate himself, blinds them to human needs; they overlook the importance of politeness and resist the requirements of society. They soon realize that they cannot live in such an atmosphere, and return to the comfort of love and affection. They discover that true sympathy (a word of many meanings!) makes one no less "sincere."

XVII   L'Epreuve
(The Test),
comedy in 1 act, T. I., 1740.

If it may seem surprising that an awkward nonconformist like Ergaste, in *Les Sincères,* was able to find an Araminte to humor him in his despair and even to marry him, what then of Lucidor in *L'Epreuve,* a fanatic of sincerity who tests Angélique's love with a detestable thoroughness that almost drives her mad? Enormously wealthy and far removed from "the mad rush for grand family alliances" (T II, 515), he is perfectly willing to marry the pretty daughter of Madame Argante (whom he has hired to run his country estate), but he is obsessed with the idea that Angélique might marry him for money. He lacks perspective on himself; he has no self-confidence. He does not recognize even the most obvious signs that Angélique loves him. He is even more introverted than Ergaste, to the point of cruelty; he may be an insensitive, an impossible husband, an extreme misanthrope. He offends Angélique until she bursts into tears and says she will "die of chagrin" (T II, 540-42). It is not always easy to take *L'Epreuve* for what it is, a hilarious comedy in which Lucidor and even Angélique are comic figures that illustrate extreme egocentricity and sensitivity. There is a grotesque range of feelings and tone which has made *L'Epreuve* one of Marivaux' most successful comedies.

Lucidor has ordered his valet, Frontin, to court her in the guise of a wealthy young suitor from Paris. Angélique hopes that the "Friend from Paris," whose arrival Lucidor announces, is really Lucidor himself, too timid to declare his love directly (Sc. 8). She is deeply upset when this friend turns out to be Frontin; she quickly excuses herself and leaves the room (T II, 529). Her mother wants to force her to accept "the gentleman from Paris" and threatens to disinherit her (T II, 535) which is rather ridiculous in view of the small dowry she can afford. Angélique recovers her wits and dispatches Frontin in one of the funniest exchanges of the play:

ANGÉLIQUE: You are a gentleman, isn't that so?
FRONTIN: That is my most brilliant accomplishment.
ANGÉLIQUE: Then you would not want to cause grief to a young girl who has never hurt you? That would be cruel and barbarous.
FRONTIN: I am the most humane of men; I have proved this to girls like you a thousand times.
ANGÉLIQUE: Isn't that wonderful? So I will tell you that I should be mortified to have to love you.

Whereupon she asks him to prove that he is a gentleman by leaving "as soon as possible" (T II, 536).

Frontin is more skillful than Arlequin in the *Jeu de l'Amour,* but this is of no avail. Besides, he has been recognized in his disguise by Lisette as the valet of Madame Dorman (Sc. 12); Lisette has the greatest difficulty calling him *vous.* Angélique needs no such proof to turn him down. Her answer, like that of Marianne facing Villot, is a resolute "no." It is interesting that in the original performance she was called Marianne.

When Lucidor finds a local peasant, Blaise, in love with Angélique and with her meagre dowry of five thousand francs, he enrolls him as a second suitor by offering him twelve thousand francs if he will make every effort to obtain her and be rejected. Maître Blaise is a shrewd rustic, like Dimas in *Le Triomphe de l'Amour*, perfectly willing to be bribed, aware that Angélique loves Lucidor, happy that Lucidor and Lisette are his witnesses when Angélique turns him down (T II, 538), for he wants to be sure to receive the money he was promised. This turns out to be harder than he bargained for, because Angélique, driven to despair by Lucidor, suddenly tells him that he is right: Yes, she has a secret lover, just as he suspects, and it is Blaise (T II, 540). Lucidor reacts in style. He not only offers Blaise twenty thousand francs dowry, but obtains Madame Argante's approval. Only when he has Angélique in tears, he relents

LUCIDOR: And if I asked for your hand and we should never leave each other as long as we live?
ANGÉLIQUE: That, at last, is talking!
LUCIDOR: You mean you love me?
ANGÉLIQUE: What else have I done all this time? (T II, 543)

Maître Blaise who had been thoroughly bewildered by Angélique's proposal and had accused her of being a typical female weathervane (T II, 540), now shows how quickly he can change. Having made sure that Lucidor is still ready to pay the twelve thousand francs originally agreed upon, he "engages himself" to Lisette whom he has courted on the sly all along, although, as he puts it, the twelve thousand francs have been much in the way (T II, 533, 542). He first had to be turned down by Angélique! Blaise is a superb creation of Marivaux.

Angélique is even more striking. Earlier versions of the theme of testing fidelity, from the *Curioso Impertinente* in *Don Quixote* (I. Chs. 33-35) to imitations by Destouches, Le Grand, and Fontenelle (1710-11), feature passive, pathetic female figures far less credible than the articulate Angélique. Even the imperceptive Lucidor is forced to recognize "a certain bitterness" in her rejection of the husbands he proffers. He asks whether she is not thankful for his many efforts. "I am thankful all right, but I am not an idiot," she tells him, and adds for Lisette's benefit: "I am sweet and good by nature; a child would show more guile than I; but if you get me mad, I promise that I will remain mad at you a thousand years! Do you understand?" (T II, 537).

Lucidor has found his match; Angélique can take care of herself. Only Madame Argante is blind enough to call her a child who does not know what she is doing (T II, 534). Therefore the abuse by Lucidor does not destroy the spirit of comedy. *L'Epreuve* is a fair battle of wits even if, at the end, Angélique breaks down in tears, since this gets Lucidor to capitulate and admit his love. Of course he is self-centered and cruel, but, as Madame de Lambert put it, "there is always cruelty in love" (*Oeuvres,* Paris, 1761, I, 363). Gabriel Marcel said that Lucidor will become a detestable husband, but is he so much worse than Ergaste in *Les Sincéres* or even Valville in *La Vie de Marianne?* They all caused great anguish to those who loved them, and so did Silvia in the *Jeu de l'Amour.* The play is not morbid; it is no study in frustration, but a superb combination of action, humor, and sentiment.

XVIII   La Commère
(The Gossip),
comedy in 1 act intended for the T. I., 1741.

The first, unsuccessful attempt at marriage of Monsieur de la Vallée, that is, Jacob, and Mademoiselle Habert, in Parts II and III of the *Paysan Parvenu,* is significantly modified for the stage in *La Commère.* In the novel, the confessor of the sisters Habert, who happens to be the one called to perform the marriage, is so resentful over losing control of the younger sister that he refuses to perform the ceremony (P, 115, n. 1). It will take place later! This scene assumed too much knowledge of past events to suit the stage version. Here a nephew of Mademoiselle Habert appears to claim an inheritance which he would lose to Jacob, and his intervention makes the marriage plan fail for good. The situation is not unlike one in *La Vie de Marianne;* there, too, a nephew, the abbé, conspires to prevent Tervire's marriage to the Baron de Sercour, an episode written the same year as *La Commère.*

Another important change is the far more important role of Madame Alain and her daughter, Agathe. Madame Alain makes one third of the responses in the entire play and lends it its title. She is very much responsible for the difficulties of the couple; she has told her suitor, Monsieur Remy, enough to alert the nephew of Mademoiselle Habert. Her warning to the maid, Javotte, to keep away the curious, is made with enough explanations to have the opposite effect. She also has the last word, as she proclaims with everyone but herself in mind: "This is what happens if one does not know enough to keep a secret!" She has not the faintest notion of the harm she does.

Agathe, who makes eyes at Jacob in the novel, shows her interest in less subtle ways on the stage. When she finds that the notary and witnesses were sent for to marry him to Mademoiselle Habert, Agathe accuses him of a breach of promise and Mademoiselle Habert, in turn, is so outraged at his infidelity that she breaks off the match herself even while the notary and witnesses stand ready to serve.

The play adds other complications. There are quarrels among those called in to assist. Javotte turns out to be a relative of Jacob who knows all about his peasant origins and reveals them to all; Javotte plays the role of Madame Dutour identifying Marianne (T II, 589 and n. 57). Thus Jacob's position is compromised. The appearance of the young nephew of Mademoiselle Habert makes the age difference of the couple even more evident and grotesque. There is more movement and interaction on the stage. Marivaux is intent on creating good comedy rather than on maintaining the detail of his novel. The result is a most effective short play; it is highly amusing. It lacks the depth of feeling in *L'Epreuve,* but it is a good parody of customs, an excellent curtain raiser frequently performed since its recent discovery by Sylvie Chevalley in the archives of the Comédie Française.

The simplest explanation why it was not performed by the Italian troupe and why Marivaux wrote no further plays for this group, even though it kept performing earlier plays of his, is furnished by his candidacy and election to the French Academy. Henceforth, he felt that he owed it to his new status, and position, to furnish plays only to the Comédie Française and to private amateur theaters. It is probably for the same reason that he abandoned the novel. He broke off *Marianne* in 1741 after Part II. Our inference is supported by an analogous attitude in the years 1736 and '37 when he refused to acknowledge authorship of the *Télémaque Travesti* and *Pharsamon* because the burlesque humor of these early compositions (they appeared in spite of his wishes) seemed inappropriate to the salons he frequented. Madame de Tencin was, after all, his powerful ally and did much to have him elected in 1742. He did not want to appear undignified, unworthy of being one of the "forty immortals."

CHAPTER 6

The Academician's View of Man

I *Address to the French Academy, 1743.*

ELECTED in December, 1742, ahead of Voltaire who was also a candidate, Marivaux' inaugural was held the following February. It was one of the most startling occasions of the kind according to d'Alembert, not so much because of what Marivaux said or of his style, but because of the outrageous reply of the Archbishop of Sens.

Marivaux took the place of the abbé d'Houtteville who had joined the Academy some twenty years earlier on the basis of his book, *The Proofs of Christianity;* he had frequently been attacked for his modern style; at the time, the abbé Pons and Marivaux (in the *Spectateur*) rallied to d'Houtteville's defense proposing that new ideas needed an appropriately modern expression and that there can be no "style" separate from the ideas it conveys. Thus, Marivaux' eulogy was addressed to an old friend and ally; his praise is sincere even though he does not hide a fundamental point of disagreement. He has little confidence in d'Houtteville's logical proofs of religion, and speaks of "the lack of faith in men's hearts which only God can overcome" (OD, 452). He implies that d'Houtteville tried to convert only man's mind whereas the appeal ought to be directed at his heart; Marivaux had insisted on this in the *Cabinet du Philosophe.*

Before discussing these issues and d'Houtteville, Marivaux' address extolls the work of the French Academy. In glowing terms he reminds his audience that the Academy is destined to preserve the spirit of France, the great tradition of Corneille, Racine, La Fontaine, and Boileau.—Molière is no accidental omission!—and the language spoken in all the courts of Europe. His comments anticipate much of Rivarol's *Discourse on the Universality of the French Language.* Marivaux speaks like the continuator of the great literature of the past and adds: "I know the value of my work . . . . False modesty here would be suspect" (OD, 449-50).

His tribute to Louis XV is one of several expressions of his loyalty; he praises the King for being so deeply moved by the loss of an outstanding minister, Fleury; a few years earlier he had shown his admiration for Fleury when he included his portrait in the scene where Marianne argues her right to marry Valville (M, 331-37 of 1737). Madame de Tencin, his unofficial sponsor, was also an ardent supporter of Fleury. Marivaux' comments are personal and pertinent; they state his mission as an author; they shy away from customary oratory.

The Archbishop of Sens is utterly unaware of this. He admits in his response that he has not read Marivaux' work and welcomes him as an accomplished gentleman more than as an author. This attitude can be partly explained by the attacks which had followed his enthusiastic welcome for Gresset (June 2, 1736); he had been told that a prelate in his position could not admit enjoying comedy; he was anxious to avoid further reproaches from Desfontaines, the *Nouvelles Ecclésiastiques,* and their allies.[1] These considerations of decorum do not excuse the severe strictures of the Archbishop; he was quite aware that he was playing the role of a censor. He even apologizes for this, but only after having proposed that literature depicts "malicious and egocentric passion" and provides dangerous models more likely to be imitated than avoided by readers. Marivaux never pretended that literature could reform the reader, but he would have disputed that it can corrupt him. It is clear that the archbishop respected the great authors of the past as little as the new candidate, and that he had no sympathy for his appeal on their behalf and on behalf of the French language. Marivaux could not help but feel hurt at the response; he wisely chose not to answer.

II Réflexions,
Comments to the French Academy, 1744.

Marivaux was to take his role in the Academy very seriously. His record of attendance remains excellent as long as he is in good health, until 1755. Periodically he contributes comments like those of 1744. They grew out of his reaction to a translation of Thucydides by d'Ablancourt. Marivaux feels that if the style is modernized as it is here, it no longer retains the "naïve" spirit of the original. In saying this, he assumes continuous progress from the childlike ages of primitive civilization to the sophisticated and cultured ideas of modern Europe (OD, 461-64). He does have some reservations: He feels, e.g., that the barbarian origins of the Roman republic do not manifest the wisdom of great civilizations that preceded it, but he sees universal progress; he believes that civilizations do not develop in isolation, but that the continuous growth of humanity fertilizes each of them.

Unfortunately such views, still popular in the Romantic era, do not lend themselves to an appreciation of Thucydides, especially if one knows as little about Greece as Marivaux. He thought that the historian belonged to a primitive epoch! Without the ability to read Greek, stylistic comparisons remain meaningless. Is Marivaux still thinking of Madame Dacier's translation of Homer? And why would Homer be "naïve"? For Thucydides the term is particularly inept, but then Jules Michelet, in the 1830's, considered all medieval literature "naïve." When Marivaux calls for a literal rendition, the phrase: "Thucydides the Athenean writes war," he fails to understand translation.

What is significant is his realization that his own world does not profit from the lessons of the past: "What use have we made of this prodigious collection of ideas handed down to us?" (OD, 463). Marivaux is a true Humanist; he does not idealize his contemporaries to the point of making them the end product of historical progress; of this his work gives ample proof. He will not twist reality to conform to a myth!

III   La Dispute
(The Argument),
comedy in 1 act, T. F., 1744.

In an almost surrealist atmosphere, Marivaux describes a "test tube" experiment in education which isolates a number of children from the world much as Rousseau isolates Emile. The "argument" is whether there is a fundamental difference between boys and girls; to find the answer, Hermiane and the Prince will observe the first confrontation of three children of each sex. Their supervisors, Mesrou and Carise, are colored and grotesque enough to belong to another species, so it can be said the children know nothing about life and society.

Eglé is first to appear. She immediately falls in love with her own image; she perceives it, for the first time in her life, in the river which traverses the wilderness shown on the stage. Soon Azor, a boy, joins her. Even though he has never set his eyes on a girl, he speaks like a courtier and suitably augments her high opinion of herself. Before long, they are in love.

A second couple, Adine and Mesrin, fall in love in a similar way, but female vanity makes the two girls desire the partner of the other boy; soon all four children will be unfaithful to their original love. In one case it is the girl, Eglé, in the other a boy, Mesrin, who first breaks with a partner. So far then, the sexes are very similar, but it is important to note that the boys, Azor and Mesrin, easily strike up a friendship, while the girls, Eglé and Adine, are hostile and jealous of each other.

Finally a third couple is introduced. They do not appear until the last scene: Meslis and Dina love each other and will remain true. Faithfulness does, after all, exist, though the pessimist could ask: Who will vouch for the future? Meslis and Dina are a sentimental supplement, a comfort for the spectator.

The Prince ironically concludes that women are no better than men. The only difference, he tells Hermiane, is that "your sex is at least more hypocritical and therefore more respectable, more preoccupied with their conscience than ours." Hermiane curtly comments: "Believe me, we don't have much to joke about! Let us leave!" (T II, 627).

It may seem unbelievable that the young semisavages with their weird names speak so well and imitate the affectations of salon society. This is part of Marivaux' fantasy setting; his realism appears when he pictures inconstancy as a fundamental human trait, at least as common as its opposite, since it touches two couples out of three. *La Double Inconstance* is an obvious parallel, but here we have no normal life situation. The play is not easy to perform. The French troupe did not do well with it; it has been presented successfully only once in recent times.

IV Le Préjugé Vaincu
(Victory over Prejudice),
comedy in 1 act, T. F., 1746.

The pride of rank and social status, so important in *Les Fausses Confidences*, weighs heavily on Angélique. She turns down Dorante even though she is in love with him. She keeps reminding herself that he is of bourgeois origin; except for that, she could not resist. It is all the more surprising as her father, the Marquis, consents to their marriage, and is so impressed with Dorante that he will allow him to marry Angélique's sister, but this is no solution; Dorante loves only Angélique. Lisette is ready to marry Dorante's valet, Lépine, but she knows that her mistress rejects Dorante in spite of her true desire; so Lisette invents obstacles for Lépine to conform to this artifice. She tells him his family does not measure up to hers. Lépine counters: It includes a trumpet player, a drummer, even an oboist, "which makes them rather noticeable" (*éclatant*—dazzling, loud, T II, 644). Lépine takes her cue and appears weeping bitter tears because his master does. He warns Angélique she may be committing double murder, for if Dorante and he leave without being married, they will arrive home like two corpses (T II, 661).

When Angélique relents and permits Lisette to marry Lépine, she is practically capitulating herself. In fact, Lisette makes Angélique's marriage a condition of her own: "Change your negative attitude and I will change mine . . . . We must have the big marriage to accompany the little one" (T II, 663). Angélique still holds out. She could marry the Baron, but then he is acceptable only to her snobbishness. When Dorante seems desperate enough to marry her sister—this is a feint as in *L'Heureux Stratagème*—Angélique gives in with this remarkable admission: "You win out over a pride which I disavow and my heart (remorse) is your vengeance" (T II, 667). She suffers for all her past pride. This is infinitely more pertinent and touching than the pompous Classical verse in Voltaire's imitation of this play, entitled *Nanine ou le Préjugé Vaincu* (1749). He had wanted to outdo Marivaux, in five acts, in Classical verse, with heroic assertions of principles and abstract truths. Characteristically his hero is masculine; he will marry Nanine for disarmingly noble motives, to prove to humanity that generosity still exists. The comparison between the two plays strikingly favors Marivaux.

Angélique is the female counterpart of Rosimond in the *Petit-Maître Corrigé:* it is another case of self-correction after everyone about has indicated in most obvious ways that she should change her mind. There is more humor here than in the earlier play and it deserves more frequent performance.

V Réflexions sur l'Esprit Humain à l'Occasion de Corneille et de Racine (Comments on Man with Reference to Corneille and Racine), *conferences to the French Academy, 1749-50.*

Scientists were often held in higher esteem than authors; scientists seemed to dominate also the salon of Madame de Tencin; this caused Marivaux once again to defend the cause of literature and *moralistes*. Science, he feels, is highly regarded only because it is specialized and hard to understand. He respects Descartes, Newton, Malebranche, and Locke (OD, 471-72), but proposes that his "science of the human heart" (OD, 476) is equally important and complex, even though its apparent deceptive simplicity makes people think they know all about it. For this reason, he tells us, the general public tends to ignore the contribution of genius on the part of those who, like himself, analyze human sentiment. For Marivaux, the heart is the cornerstone not only of passion or love, but of reason.

In passing he comments on the almost miraculous achievement of the child who learns his own language (OD, 479); then on the equally surprising effect of social pressure which favors certain types of learning. If mathematics were essential for social success, no one would speak of his incapacity in the field (OD, 490); the motivation the acrobat's son receives from his father, goes a long way to his attaining competence (OD, 488-89).

When Marivaux defines the primary task of literature in terms of psychological analysis, he may startle the modern reader who holds to an aesthetic ideal and wants no part of the social sciences. We must remember that Marivaux is trying to formulate a theory to buttress his fascination with people and their motives; that he is doing so at a time when psychology did not exist as a discipline, and that there were not even adequate terms for describing its phenomena. Marivaux' interest does not preclude a superb feeling for language and for literary form. Ever since 1719, he has been discussing the relationship between style and content, advocating that the first is a function of the second, that style is the most adequate expression of the ideas and observations the author wishes to make, and so he returns once again to his great models, Corneille and Racine, who distinguished themselves in analyzing man, his motives and problems, and whose work must be taken as seriously as that of the "geometricians" from Descartes to Malebranche. His comments elaborate on the theme which he had briefly stated in his inaugural address of 1743; he is still trying to convince his fellow Academicians of the mission of literature, and of his own. He does not want to be known as a facile entertainer, but as a serious artist who continues a great French tradition.

VI   La Colonie
(The Colony),
comedy in 1 act for the amateur stage of the Count of Clermont, 1750 (cf. T II, 795).

In 1729 Marivaux produced his third island play, *La Nouvelle Colonie,* in three acts, on the Italian stage. It was a complete failure and remained unpublished. Its subject, Aristophanes' *Lysistrata,* was treated far more coyly than in the original. The women aspire to equal rights without mentioning the shocking idea of withdrawing from relations with men; they enter the political scene only after the male delegates

(Timagène represents the nobility, Sorbin the common people) have enacted a law to protect them; it provides that only polite requests will be honored. At this point Silvia, loved by Timagène, and Madame Sorbin may take over, or at least try to do so, for things work out very badly. Hermocrate is elected to restore order. He outlaws Timagène and the Sorbins, and restores the power to men. Women will rule only in the domain of love, as we can see from the ballet that follows. Only a summary of the action, in the *Mercure,* and the ballet have come down to us.

In the version of 1750, the action is much condensed. Silvia becomes Arthénice, Arlequin will be called Persinet, since we no longer deal with the actors of the Italian troupe. Persinet stems from a fairy tale of Madame d'Aulnoy, *Gracieuse et Persinet,* which is indeed a source of the play and where we also find a young couple unable to marry because of an impossible mother. Here it will be Madame Sorbin who wants to outlaw love to establish women's power. In this new version, Hermocrate need not exile anyone; an attack of savages upsets the regime of the women; they need men to defend them and therefore return to the household.

We can see how far Marivaux stands from women's liberation, but there are a few daring passages. One woman protests that, from the cradle on, women are told:

You are good for nothing; don't get involved, just be good! Our mothers heard and believed this. We repeat it after them and our ears are beaten down from such evil talk. Since we are sweet and tend to be lazy, we can be led like little sheep. (T II, 684-85)

This passage is exceptional. Most of the time the women are silly, even absurd. Madame Sorbin wants to do away with love; she would have women make themselves ugly (T II, 681, 688-89). Arthénice, who represents the nobility, is not much better. She prides herself that women "have corrected the ferocity of men's souls" and adds: "Without us the earth would be but an abode of savages; one could not even call them human" (T II, 686-87). This is grotesque in view of the attack by savages which brings her power to its downfall. Another lady aims to "do away with the suppers" of salon society *(ibid.)* which is, at best, incongruous. When Persinet is willing to move some benches, so that his beloved Dina, the daughter of Madame Sorbin, will not have to touch them with her delicate hands (T II, 684), we can only wonder why Marivaux has become so precious. There is no comic relief at all, unless one considers the exaggerations of Madame Sorbin to be funny.

La Colonie seems particularly dated. Too many of the demands of women that seemed absurd to Marivaux have become realities. The collapse of their power when savages attack merely shows that Marivaux had no idea how women lived in the frontier societies of his own day, e.g., on the Mississippi. In *La Dispute* he had shown that men and women were equal in fickleness, if not also in vanity; in *L'Ile de la Raison* he called them the weaker sex, to be protected by having to declare their love before the men. In *La Colonie*, Marivaux disputes that Arthénice and Madame Sorbin could ever rule as well as men; the experience of Hermocrate is irreplaceable and they must call on him for help. Marivaux has gone no further than Fénelon's plea for women's education.

VII   *Lectures to the French Academy and Essays, 1751-54.*

According to the abbé Raynal, Marivaux' commentaries read to the French Academy were uneven and less and less appreciated (OD, 465, n. 2, 714-15) and the fragments that were published in the *Mercure* may not correspond to what he said; *Le Miroir* will contain material which he may originally have wanted to read to the Academy. Marivaux is not at his best when he reduces live situations to principles, yet this is what he felt called upon to present to the august body. His theory of government is interesting, but less striking and concise than the thoughts of Montesquieu in the *Persian Letters* or the *Dialogue of Sylla and Eucrate,* where we can find many parallels.

Two pages of *Réflexions* (1751, OD, 501-2) reexamine the infinite possibilities for progress and human development. Marivaux stresses that courage can become temerity, generosity can turn into waste, study can be useless effort; it is all right to be "infinitely" good, generous, and the like, but excess will negate the basic virtue. It all leads up to the sensitive question of insight and wit *(esprit),* for Marivaux had often been reproached by critics, including the Archbishop of Sens (responding to the inaugural address), for having gone too far in this direction. When Marivaux advocates the just measure, there are undertones of a passionate self-defense.

This applies equally to the first section of the *Réflexions sur les Hommes (Comment on Man,* 1751, OD, 509-10) where he returns to this theme: "Too much ignorance steeps a people in barbarism; too much experience makes it clever but perverted; the golden mean provides for a better life" (OD, 509). There follow comments on national pride, a source of greatness, and individual pride, a necessity for man: The king's best subject will be proud and independent (OD, 510). We can sense the personal commitment of Marivaux; he is describing himself.

The *Réflexions sur les Romains (Comments on the Romans,* 1751, OD, 504-5) compare the establishment of empires in Persia, Macedonia, and Rome. Marivaux believes that it becomes increasingly difficult to be an absolute ruler, for it is less easy to deceive the more educated peoples into abandoning freedom. This somewhat simplistic faith in progress and enlightenment is further developed in the *Réflexions sur les Hommes* (see above), where Marivaux examines the role of Oliver Cromwell. He needed "skillful extravagance" to acquire "the courage to apply certain means," ruthless modes of control and military power. Here "the wise man with his extensive understanding of conditions would have perished" (OD, 510-12). Marivaux recognizes that Cromwell established his regime with great skill, but he is horrified by the results, just like the abbé Prévost and other contemporaries. Cromwell is the arch-villain. The example in many ways runs counter to Marivaux' general theory of progress, for if freedom could be so effectively suppressed in the seventeenth century, where is the advance of freedom he postulates? In fact, he is not claiming freedom rules; he believes, or hopes that it becomes ever more difficult to suppress.

The idea recurs a third time in *L'Education d'un Prince (Educating a Prince,* 1754, OD, 515-28), written for the birth of Louis XVI. The dialogue of a young ruler, Théodose, with his mentor, Théophile, comments on absolute power, which may in earlier times have produced "dizzy" tyranny, but which is now subject to the rule of reason that prevents the most adverse results (OD, 522). We now have safeguards: individual rights and freedom.

The most important lesson Théophile wants to inculcate in the young ruler is that his best subjects are free men who dare act independently. Two stories, which make up almost half the essay, illustrate this point. The first is a comparison between an amiable flatterer, Sostène, and a proud individualist, Philante, whose honesty must be preferred. The second is an oriental tale. A king could not convince his intemperate son to respect the rights of his people. To teach him a lesson, the king waited for the birth of his grandson, then had the infant child of a slave placed beside the newborn. The young prince is terrified, for he cannot tell which child is his, whereupon the king identifies the right child, but has taught his son that royal blood lends no natural distinction (OD, 520-21, 523-26).

The democratic, individualistic, and optimistic strains in Marivaux' thought are matched by his fundamental loyalty to his king. Théophile tells the young ruler:

There is nothing radical in what I say, no temerity, nor do I assume the airs of a *philosophe*. You will never suspect me of wanting to abridge your prerogatives .... These are dear to me because *you* have them; they are sacred to me because they are yours not only by the right of men, but of God; need I add that all types of thought, the most absurd, impertinent, and unjust, is to belittle the majesty of those institutions which are absolutely essential to the State. (OD, 522-23)

Thus Marivaux upholds the divine right of kings in all sincerity. He sees in it no stricture on his freedom as a political being or a thinker. Théophile goes as far as to say: "Let the ruler hate me so long as his rule is safe, let him be unjust to me as long as the people love him" (OD, 518); at which point Théodose objects that he would never hate his best subject or treat him unjustly; he has learned his lesson!

VIII   Le Miroir
(The Mirror),
a philosophical essay, 1755.

In a world which "no geographer ever described," we find goddess Nature. She wears a diadem with two mirrors, one reflecting "the hidden essence of matter," the other reflecting the states of man's soul and thought (OD, 534-35). It is the second mirror which captures the author's attention.

He discovers in it the image of many works of literature and philosophy which have influenced him, the powerful genius of Corneille, the incomparable elegance of Racine who moves his audience to compassion, the "admirable frenzy of sentiment" in Crébillon's *Rhadamiste et Zénobie* (OD, 539). We find Fontenelle's idea that Newton built his edifice on the outdated but essential genius of Descartes (OD, 536), but he shows little enthusiasm for Locke. Marivaux approves of Malebranche, who sees all in God; he repays Voltaire's insults with compliments and expresses his appreciation of the *Henriade* and *Zaïre* (OD, 536-39).

As Frédéric Deloffre points out, *Le Miroir* constitutes a very incomplete list of influences on Marivaux. It omits Cervantes, Pascal, the *Lettres de la Religieuse Portugaise* by Guilleragues, as well as Dufresny, Dancourt, and many other essential sources, like the *Illustres*

Françaises by Robert Challes. Furthermore, Marivaux devotes two-thirds of his text to three digressions. The first concerns the ill effect of fame that arouses jealousy: A good author like Chapelain dared no longer be himself, once he had achieved success, for fear of being attacked by critics (OD, 537-38). It shows how hard it was for Marivaux to bear their charges. The second digression contains an apology for La Motte and praise for Helvétius whose personal kindness greatly aided Marivaux. There is reference to his unpublished work, *De l'Esprit* (OD, 539-41). La Motte is overrated, once again a testimony of personal loyalty, though Marivaux admits that La Motte was more a man of reason than of sentiment. The third digression (OD, 542-49) takes up issues of the Battle of the Books. Marivaux still resents that authors of antiquity are preferred to contemporaries. For the sake of argument, he assumes that if men had always been that foolish, even Helen of Troy would not have been admired in her own day. Years hence, the authors living now will become the battle-ax used to denigrate the authors of the future. Once again, Marivaux stresses the idea of progress; he believes in the infallible increase of ideas and concedes only that there are periods when good taste is lost and men are unable to benefit from the accumulation of human wisdom (OD, 549). His philosophical optimism is almost unlimited and extends far beyond what we might accept. His ridiculing Homer, Euripides, and Sophocles, in that order (OD, 542), to us betrays ignorance and lack of appreciation. It must be understood that Marivaux dislikes these authors mostly because their devotees swear by them in order not to recognize efforts like his own.

IX   La Femme Fidèle
(The Faithful Wife),
comedy in 1 act for the amateur stage of the Comte de Clermont, the Théâtre de Berny, 1755.

For all his mockery of Homer, Marivaux draws his next play from the story of Ulysses, which had already served him in the *Télémaque Travesti;* he recounts the return of a long-lost husband who finds his wife besieged by a suitor, just one to suit modern taste (cf. Doña Mencia in *Gil Blas* by Lesage). The Marquis returns with his servant, Frontin, from ten years of captivity among the pirates of North Africa. The shrewd and amusing gardener, Colas, recognizes them behind their disguise and beards, but he promises not to give them away while the Marquis "tests" the fidelity of his wife (cf. *L'Epreuve*). The Marquis decides not to reveal his identity until he is sure she will not marry Dorante, who is pressuring her; the parallel case is that of Lisette pursued by Jeannot.

Colas and the other servants keep this comedy of sentiment from becoming tearful. Even Dorante adds an element of humor: The Marquis refuses to hand over a portrait of the Marquise. As the best friend of her long-lost husband, he asserts that no one but she herself was to possess it; whereupon Dorante interjects: "Your memory is excellent indeed!" Dorante has already found out that this visitor knows too much about the Marquis to be who he says he is (T II, 721). When, in the end, the Marquis and his wife are happily reunited, Dorante concludes: "No one is more out of place around here than I" (T II, 731).

Is the Marquis not excessive in demanding that his wife reject Dorante without knowing that he, her husband, is alive? Marivaux would reply: No more so than Silvia in the *Jeu de L'Amour* who forces Dorante to offer marriage to her, disguised as a servant maid, or than Lucidor in *L'Epreuve*.

The situation in *La Femme Fidèle* is grotesque, for Dorante has been "consoling" the Marquise for two years while living near her "in utmost respect" and she, in turn, has thought of him only as a "gentleman" friend nice to have around, not a potential husband (T II, 729). The situation of Penelope has been transformed into an utterly moral, platonic relationship. The arrival of a supposed friend of her husband is enough to move her to tears. Her mother, Madame Argante, objects to the unreal sentimentality; she feels that it is time that the Marquise remarry and blames him for upsetting her: "Are you glad that you are making my daughter weep? Your manners are all too Algerian!" (T II, 721). She has a point, but Marivaux does not consider it barbarous to make another suffer for love. In the *Jeu*, Dorante thanks Silvia for putting him to a test; in *L'Epreuve*, Angélique is all too happy to marry Lucidor. Similarly, the joy of the Marquise knows no bounds when the stranger removes his beard and turns out to be her husband!

Only the four principal roles of *La Femme Fidèle* are extant, along with bare indications of cues. Let us hope that the roles of Frontin, Lisette, and Jeannot will be rediscovered.

X Félicie,
comedy in 1 act, written for the T. F., 1757.

L'Ecole des Mères and *La Mère Confidente,* among other plays, revolved around the conflict between generations. The problem of Félicie is related: Can the young girl accept the advice of her elders? In the allegorical setting, these are represented by the Fairy Hortense, Diana, and Modesty. Lucidor is trying to wean Félicie from their influence; he is more dangerous than Climal, in *La Vie de Marianne,* for he is young and attractive. Félicie would just as soon "disregard the pitfalls" which Modesty keeps talking about (T II, 744). Her foolhardy desire to savor experience drives the three guardian spirits away (T II, 750, 854). When they return, she alienates them again (T II, 758). Félicie seems lost. She is saved only by her fright when Lucidor tries to draw her forcefully towards him:

Heavens! Where are you taking me? Where am I? What will become of me? My conscience, their absence, and my love terrify me. (She cries out:) Oh! dear Modesty, dear companion, where are you? Where are they? (T II, 759)

A crisis situation was required to determine the heroine to choose virtue in defiance of her gay surroundings, the dazzling lover, and her sensuous desires. There is a powerful strain of pessimism in this allegory, a realistic appraisal of human motives. The success of the final, desperate resolve of Félice to reject Lucidor never seems assured.

XI   Les Acteurs de Bonne Foi
(Actors in Good Faith),
comedy in one act, 1757.

Félicie and *L'Amante Frivole (A Frivolous Girl in Love),* a play now lost, were submitted to the Comédie Française in 1757; both were read but not performed by the troupe. *Les Acteurs de Bonne Foi* was probably submitted directly to the *Conservateur,* the review that published the play, for Merlin jokes, when he cannot produce his comedy, that he is "reduced" to the sad fate of having it printed (T II, 782). Such lack of success and resignation on the part of the author should not lead us to overlook the value of Marivaux' late plays, especially *Les Acteurs* and *La Provinciale,* where he explores new resources of comedy.

The new theme in *Les Acteurs* is the world as a stage. There are two plays within the play. The characters are at the service of Madame Amelin who wants to be amused. First it is up to the masterful servant, Merlin, to organize her entertainment. Merlin quickly imagines a plot which suits his secret desires, for he will flirt with Colette who loves the young farmer, Blaise, and will do so right in front of Blaise, also in front of Lisette who hopes to marry Merlin. The result can be expected. Blaise becomes desperate because Colette enjoys the attentions of her distinguished lover. In one performance he shrieked and jumped into the air in his rage, landing with tremendous noise with his sabots on the wooden stage; he seemed so absurd that the audience could not feel sorry for him and laughed uproariously, and yet his antics are a pathetic protest against Merlin, playing with his feelings. Meanwhile Lisette vents her jealousy and anger in more articulate ways. Ironically, it is not because Blaise and Lisette are too involved to act that Merlin cannot continue his performance, but because Madame Argante will tolerate no performance in her house; so Madame Amelin must look for other sources of amusement.

She will have a play to spite all! She pretends that her wealthy friend, Araminte, is to marry Eraste in the place of the girl he loves, Angélique. Araminte is quite a few years older that Eraste. Their marriage would seem as unseemly as that of Jacob and Mademoiselle Habert in the *Paysan Parvenu.* Like Mademoiselle Habert who will not admit being fifty, Araminte protests that she is being maligned: She is not forty as yet, just thirty-nine and a half (T II, 790).

The joke is on Eraste, Araminte's nephew, for he was all in favor of Merlin's comedy. Obviously he is no longer amused now that the merriment continues at his expense. He must suffer for quite a while, for Madame Amelin continues the pretense right to the end, when it is discovered that the marriage contract is drawn in the name of Eraste and Angélique. As in *L'Heureux Stratagème,* the "happy ending" is preceded by great anguish. It seems more cruel in this case, for it does not serve the purpose of bringing the lovers together.

It becomes evident that "the actors in good faith" are characters led by the nose by those of bad faith who seek amusement. This is illustrated first on the level of servants, then of the masters. The trick works in both cases; it is easy to play with the feelings of others. Even Madame Argante, Angélique's mother, a serious, all too literal-minded but not unappealing person, is fooled, and so, of course, are her daughter and Eraste. When Madame Argante finds out that her daughter will be married after all, she exclaims:

Ah! Ah! I guessed it. You were putting on a comedy and I have been had for a fool. Well, let us sign the contract, but you certainly are nasty people! (T II, 790)

An innocent little game like that of Silvia in the last part of the *Jeu de l'Amour?* Not really, for too many participants are led to despair: Blaise, Lisette, Eraste, Angélique, Madame Argante. They are the tools of Madame Amelin and of Araminte, or of Merlin. Most everyone is like Lisette who first shouts her approval: "How I love comedy!" but when Merlin explains he will pretend to love Colette, is forced to add: "This better not go too far, for I cannot stand that kind of thing, I warn you!" (T II, 771). Everyone laughs at others and protests when the tables are turned, a pessimistic picture of social relations! After all, Madame Amelin comes close to breaking up two marriages. Scars will be left in many hearts.

For this reason we can hardly speak of a happy ending. As Madame Argante puts it in protest against the supposed marriage of Araminte with Eraste: "Such proceedings are justified only in a dream-world, certainly only there, and the performance of your miserable little comedy will destroy it" (T II, 785-86). But she is caught and forced to act in it herself. Marivaux suggests we all play with each other to pass the time, to create or destroy a dream as the case may be; we all will act for Madame Amelin in order to escape, to be entertained, or wrest the wand from a fairy queen, like Arlequin "polished by love."

XII La Provinciale
(The Country Wife in Paris),
comedy in one act for the amateur stage of the Comte de Clermont, 1761.

There is no longer any question; *La Provinciale* is by Marivaux. The play may be a revision of *L'Auberge Provinciale,* a comedy of 1735, now lost, and reworked as was *La Nouvelle Colonie* of 1729, to produce *La Colonie* of 1750.

Madame Riquet, a wealthy widow, has bought an estate and calls herself La Marquise de la Thibaudière. She has recently arrived in Paris and befriended Madame Lépine. The latter conspires with a crook, who pretends to nobility and is known as Le Chevalier, to buy him a fictitious regiment for thirty thousand francs. The situation is grotesque, for the Chevalier, who is after the money of the Marquise, has as little claim to the title as she does. This is social comedy, more crudely funny than any other by Marivaux, an attempt to tackle new themes and techniques.

The Chevalier offers to educate the country widow in the ways of Parisian gallantry and finds in her a most willing disciple. Indeed, she welcomes his advances with an almost wanton openness. There is a parallel with Félicie whom Lucidor wants to seduce, but the Marquise is all too eager and the Chevalier interested only in money (T II, 815, cf. 579). She explains: "I come from the country of crass ignorance" and is so forward so she will not seem "the most stupid and idiotic of women." She tells him: "You please me more than you deserve!" (T II, 813, 819, 821). Marivaux' humor has become broad, as in the *Précieuses Ridicules;* the play lacks the light wit and sparkle that have been his distinguishing mark, though the essential features of his language remain and identify the play.

Lisette, the maid of the Marquise, who now pretentiously calls herself Cathos, is as deluded as her mistress. She encourages her in the course to perdition and falls in love with La Ramée, the valet and associate of the Chevalier. Like him, La Ramée pursues only money but he is more humane: "What a shame," he says, "that I treat her like a scoundrel." Lisette suspects she is not his only love: "Do I have rivals?" and La Ramée: "Paris teems with them like an ant-heap!" (T II, 830).

The Chevalier, La Ramée, and Madame Lépine, in close association, draw in accomplices like the "unknown lady" who is supposed to vie with the Marquise for the honor of advancing the money to the Chevalier. The crooks are well organized. The list of characters seems open-ended as the circle of swindlers widens and entraps the Marquise.

At this point there arrive Monsieur Lormeau, a country cousin, his friend Derval, a worthy match for the "Marquise," and two of Derval's sisters. They reinforce the troops of the good cause, but are as unwelcome as Madame Dutour who revealed Marianne's bourgeois origins. Lormeau does just that; furthermore, he unmasks the "Chevalier" as the son of a local attorney. One has the impression that rival armies are clashing. The forces of honesty confound the crooks and disperse them. Lormeau leads the charge. The fortune of Madame Riquet, soon to be Madame Derval, is safe! The rescue came in the nick of time! Vanity was hard to defeat; in Marivaux there is no comfortable triumph of good over evil. At the age of seventy-three, he has not lost his touch. He can still renew himself and make an important contribution to a new genre, bourgeois drama.

CHAPTER 7

The Art of Marivaux

I Style

THE distinguishing mark of literature is structure and form, the author's organization of his ideas, and the means he chooses to convey them. Marivaux was superbly conscious of this art, more than most of his contemporaries. He asks that his work be judged in accord with the purpose he proposes for himself. In the preface to his first novel, which is essentially a tale of adventure imitated from La Calprenède, he states his original objective, that of moving the reader; his novel will merit approval only if it succeeds in stirring in the reader the feelings the author seeks to express. In order to gain critical distance not only from the authors who inspire him, but from the society he tries to analyze, he soon adopts the device of parody; he establishes a comic and often paradoxical relationship between his account and the one he leans on, be it a text of Cervantes, Fénelon, La Motte's Homer, or *A Thousand and One Nights,* to mention the most evident sources of subsequent works. Marivaux merges description with fantasy, realistic concern for the issues of his day with burlesque contrasts. He analyzes while doing all he can to amuse his reader, for he knows that this is the way to retain his attention.

The emphasis is on expressing or clearly implying his own feelings, his particular personality and frame of mind. In this manner Marivaux comes to abandon the model of French Classicism, in novels and verse satire as well as on the stage. He shifts, if not the subject matter, the tone and focus of the work. He realizes that he continues a grand tradition, but also that he can do so effectively only if he avoids close imitation. His failure to discuss and refer to Molière is striking!

He also adopts an individual mode of expression, a style suited to his intellectual humor, often involving paradox, e.g., when proverbs are cited or assertions made that could be true under other circumstances, but in his work merely denote the illusions or the character who makes these statements. Precepts of Cicero and Quintilian, taught in classes in rhetoric and proposed as universally applicable models, could not serve his quest for originality. Marivaux would not accept an established code of good writing imposed by the authority of Classical antiquity. Indeed, he was a resolute partisan of the Moderns who postulated that the genius of antiquity did not transcend that of modern authors and that each period, or even each piece of literature, derived its stylistic requirements from its particular subject and purpose. These arguments were aimed at the Ancients ever intent to emulate Classical authors and at critics who attacked Marivaux because he departed from established standards and practice. These critics forced him to clarify his position; his replies constitute an impressive body of sensitive, critical commentary that illuminates his creative effort.

The progress of the early Marivaux can be identified with three states: Imitations, though with some originality, as *Le Père Prudent* and *Les Effets Surprenants de la Sympathie;* then the style of parody *(style travesti),* which includes the hilarious scenes with Cliton-Pharsamon in the *Don Quichotte Moderne (Pharsamon),* analogous episodes in rollicking popular speech, in the *Télémaque Travesti,* new perspectives, the individual psychology of the travellers who make up an oriental tale in *La Voiture Embourbée,* contemporary literary issues incorporated in a mock epic conceived in the tradition of Scarron, his unsuccessful *Homère Travesti.* In each instance, the parody is also a form of criticism, a critique of unreal settings, human folly, cruelty and intolerance, directed not at the authors who served as models, but at contemporary practice and circumstance. The works of this second period do introduce a realistic view of society, an increasingly pertinent analysis of character. Therefore, when Marivaux finds his true style, first in the essays beginning in 1717, then in plays, finally also in novels, his departures are less radical than they might at first seem. There is a great deal of continuity in his work. The essential function of "reflections," the author's speculations, or those of his characters, the role of sentiment but also rational analysis, all this can be discovered even in his earliest publications.

Marivaux' appeal remains twofold, to the emotions and to intelligence. This leads him before Rousseau to the concept of "the reason of the heart." His characters act, then seek to discover their motives; often they possess, in addition, an intuitive awareness of the truth, as, for instance, Madame de Miran; she understands Marianne's despair immediately (M 415). In a different context, the contrast between feeling and thinking produces comic paradox. The girl who uses her mind to "catch up with her heart," i.e., trying to understand what she has done, comically restates a basic mode of action of many characters. Such a technique saved Marivaux from bombastic restatement of the commonplace or evident principle, the great fault of Voltaire's tragedies. Rational analysis in Marivaux serves not popular edification, but illustrates the assumptions, or delusions, of the particular speaker in each case. Marivaux aims to amuse while flattering the reader's, or spectator's understanding; he believes that wisdom, pedantically proclaimed, is ineffective. He underlines this point by presenting a number of intolerable pedants in his plays, representatives of the Ancients and their unrealistic world-view.

We have used the term, "paradox" to qualify an early stylistic form in Marivaux' work *(style travesti)* and the contrasts it involves between the model and its burlesque imitation, between fiction and reality. In the later work, we find paradox without a literary crutch. There are, essentially, two types: statements to be disproved by their context or by what is to happen, and statements that are self-contradictory.

The first type, the more frequent, makes it difficult to define Marivaux' ideas or point of view by giving brief citations. Out of context, his statements may be completely misleading. The disillusionment with marriage in the two *Surprises* is so much self-deception. Silvia, who in *La Double Inconstance* proclaims it is better to remain poor than to accept a wealthy, unhappy marriage, will be happy with the Prince. In *Le Dénouement Imprévu,* the schemes of Mademoiselle Argante come to naught because she falls in love. The supposedly devoted mother, in *La Mère Confidente,* who would protect her daughter from the advances of Dorante, accepts this suitor because he promises not to elope with her; Dorante, on the other hand, who tried to advance his cause by talking about his wealthy uncle, finds that this uncle is the major obstacle to his marriage. Ergaste is not only too young and hale to die and leave him an inheritance, but he turns out to be his rival in love. In *Les Acteurs de Bonne Foi,* the joke is on all who are "of good faith." The title turns out to be a paradox as do many others beginning with the very first play where the father, neither foresighted nor equitable as is claimed, is ill-advised in opposing his daughter's inclination.

The second type of paradox contains the elements of confusion in a single statement. A good part of the *Télémaque Travesti* relies on this kind of humor, e.g., when praise of a faithful wife is followed by the interjection: "But the uncertainty of it all." Marivaux' use of the term, *honnête,* involves constant puns on its contradictory meanings, "honest, honorable, polite, gentlemanly," or only seemingly so. The

Prince, in *La Double Inconstance,* is called noble and sensitive to the feelings of others even while he is engaged in seduction. Similarly Climal, parading as a devout benefactor to the poor, tells Marianne that she "is pleasing" to him; she blushes and pretends not to know why (M, 31). The buffoonery of many an Arlequin, the crass self-interest of a character like Dimas in *Le Triomphe de l'Amour,* join supposedly sincere offers of help and service with reminders such as: "Always remember that my own gain is at the end of it all" (T I, 924). The world is built on self-interest; Marivaux knows it like La Fontaine and La Rochefoucauld.

The "reflections" of Marivaux' characters who philosophize, or muse from their known, biased point of view, are humorous because they are ambiguous and paradoxical. Marianne's proposition that one no longer follows moral principle when one leads others to believe one has none, merely means that one must draw the line somewhere, and is used to justify her previous actions which lead Climal to believe that she might become his mistress. Her statement is all but a cornerstone of ethics.

Reflections may be analytical comments or emotional reactions. They shift the literary objective from the telling of plot to the illustration of character; as such they become an end in themselves and, consequently, are the essential element of Marivaux' technique. It took him longer to write his two major novels than the time-span they encompass! Hostile critics mocked him for this. They failed to understand that his objective was to "penetrate" the soul of his characters, not to be their historian.

In *Pharsamon* he had explained how a minute detail (*un rien*) can become a matter of extended speculation (OJ, 562). What is commented upon is as important as what is omitted in defining the frame of mind of those who speak. Marivaux makes the subtle point when he contrasts the couples he portrays in the *Surprise* and in *Les Serments Indiscrets* (in the preface to this play): Two of the young people love each other without knowing it, the other two have staked their honor on not giving in to passion. In both cases they do not mention love, in both cases their actions belie their feelings; since their concerns and degree of insight differ so greatly, their parallel comments take on very different meanings.

The essential element in such distinctions is "finesse," precise definition, be it through reflections or ordinary dialogue. The style must be appropriate to what is implied. This is why Frédéric Deloffre defines "marivaudage" as an amusing play with ideas, serious in intent, a play with language where new concepts demand a new and precise terminology (D, 499; OD, 383). This precision is so important because the technique of paradox implies more than it states. Marivaux maintains that subjects lose meaning and beauty if every aspect is explained; objects become ugly when placed in a blinding light. Sufficient clarity is all that is required. The subject must be presented clearly, "in the utmost degree of meaning and truth," but without belabored explanations (OD, 54-57).

This statement of literary principle of 1719 will be further refined. In 1722 Marivaux advises authors not to mold their thought on others, to resemble only themselves, to maintain their peculiar mentality (OD, 149). In 1734 he insists on "finesse" as the tool which permits the author to penetrate his subject and arrive at "the exact figuration" of his ideas (OD, 386). In 1755 he once again speaks of his technique of psychological investigation and calls it "the science of the human heart" (OD, 475). While hostile critics referred to Marivaux' desperate search for wit (OD, 145) and excessive *préciosité*, he stresses the relevance of his distinctions. He has been proven right. The amusing contrast between what is stated and what is meant is most effective.

There are, of course, instances where Marivaux is precious, where modern taste differs from his. In *La Colonie*, Persinet moves benches so that Lina need not use her delicate little hands (T II, 684). In *Le Jeu*, Dorante tells Silvia she need not say, "I wish," for her wishes will be obeyed without command (T I, 807). However, these instances of polite speech were not what bothered Marivaux' contemporaries. They objected to the very distinctions which make Marivaux the great author he is, his portrayal of individual psychology and attitudes, his requirement that the author cling to the individuality that makes him original (*la singularité d'esprit qui nous est échue*). This statement seemed so grotesque to Desfontaines that he did not even explain why he thought it to be absurd. Fortunately we understand Marivaux better than Desfontaines; we are no longer passionately engaged in the Battle of the Books and agree that Marivaux was not espousing a modern fad, like the one he condemned in *Le Bilboquet*, but rather the renewal of the Classical tradition, of the psychological investigation of the tragedies of Corneille and Racine, of the commentary concerning man from Pascal to Malebranche.

Literary technique mattered to Marivaux; he devoted his entire effort to his creations, to the intellectual life. What he calls his laziness (OD, 117, 441-44) is merely the use of leisure to observe, meditate, discuss, and then write. He chose this kind of life in preference to any other, especially to polemics that filled so much of Voltaire's time.

Marivaux' effort to individualize his style, each aspect of truth, to let every character speak for himself, is unique in his day; there result a great variety of styles; they distinguish not only between individuals, but between the moods of the same person. We have discussed some of these in *La Vie de Marianne,* the language of sobs, of strong emotion, rhetorical apostrophe, meditation, reflection. The burlesque speech of his servants and peasants is a convention of the French stage since Molière, an approximation of popular speech in the Paris region modified by contact with the upper classes, but partly also a rendition of the idiosyncrasies of an individual Arlequin, Trivelin, Dimas, personalized like the jargon of an Hortensius or the Gascon accent of Rosimond in *Le Petit-Maître Corrigé.* Characters express their moods, their particular purposes, while the reader, or spectator, smiles at their modes of thought and their delusions. Marivaux is conscious of his multiple purposes, capable of great variety of expression, paradoxically humorous, in constant search of the individual portrait through lively, humorous dialogue and descriptions appropriate to the speaker in whose mouth he places them. This makes him one of the great stylists of French literature.

II *Themes*

Each of the major themes of Marivaux deserves a critical study as extensive as our discussion of his work. Mrs. Brady's *Love in the Theater of Marivaux* is an example to the point, but even this searching, intelligent discussion does not preclude further investigations from different perspectives. A wealth of quotations could be drawn from Marivaux' work to illustrate each theme. We shall mention only a few examples in each case. If the reader keeps these themes in mind while perusing Marivaux' work, he can easily compile his own anthology and observe the author's evolution. The danger lies in taking the views of characters to be those of Marivaux. We must take account of his implications, of the twists of wit and irony.

A. *Reason and Unreason*

Utopia is pictured in Marivaux' first novel, *Les Effets Surprenants de la Sympathie* (OJ, 282-90). Its absence in *Le Télémaque Travesti,* where the reader and Marivaux' characters expect to encounter it by analogy to Fénelon's *Bétique,* is all the more significant. Jokingly it is said that utopia must have vanished from the earth (OJ, 823-24). Indeed, violence and injustice dominate the novel; the inhumanity of the religious wars is evident. A temporary truce brought about by the hero and his mentor is grotesque, and precarious at that (OJ, 327-32, 347-49). The rule of reason is no easy objective. If Marivaux believes that man has progressed beyond the mentality of Homer's killers (X, 564), he is equally aware that it is difficult to be "reasonable," i.e., aware of the needs of others, as the term is defined in *L'Ile de la Raison* where servants understand more quickly than their masters what reform is expected of them, and where a philosopher and a poet are too self-centered to recover their human greatness. The reform to the condition of reason is possible and so Marivaux clings to an idealistic optimism, but it is difficult; there is the danger of relapse; we see a healthy realism that balances utopian thought.

Marivaux did not greatly modify this view in later years. The youths in *La Dispute* are as likely to be vain and fickle as not; evil is close to triumph in *La Provinciale*. Besides, many a happy ending implies the danger of relapse and disappointment, the resurgence of egocentricity which defeats love. One "lucky stratagem" gives little assurance for the future; one fop may be turned into a desirable husband, but another in the same play is unchanged (Dorante in *Le Petit-Maître Corrigé*). There are villains like Lelio in *La Fausse Suivante* or Frédéric in *Le Prince Travesti*. We have noted the crisis of pessimism in 1723-24 when Marivaux lost his wife after having lost a fortune; we have also noted the irony implied in the rise of Marianne and Jacob; their supposed virtue is being consistently rewarded. What are we to say of Ergaste in *Les Sincères* and Lucidor's even more extreme behavior in *L'Epreuve?* The desperate need for reassurance and understanding of these two characters inflicts a great deal of suffering on others and is hardly a "reasonable" attitude.

The more closely we look at Marivaux' characters, the more remote his basic optimism will appear. There is progress. The "barbarous" heartlessness of masters is eradicated on the Island of Slaves (T I, 521) while, on the Island of Reason, most Europeans profit from the lessons in humility (T I, 605). Several discourses to the French Academy bring out the idea of progress, though Marivaux concedes that taste can be lost and the lessons of the past unheeded (OD, 546-49). He believes that princes can be educated to become enlightened rulers, or pretends to believe this in the hope his essay will make the dream come true (OD, 515f). Still, unreason intervenes all too frequently to consider his work in rosy light.

There are, first, extreme cases of violence and injustice, some in his first novel of traditional hue, due to fated passion; the rape of Bastille in *La Voiture Embourbée* is pictured in the same vein, also the Mirski episode of *Le Spectateur* (no. 9-11) where the villain is foiled. Most of the later protrayals are seen in the more humane light of ambiguous character and human foibles. The seduction of Silvia by the Prince in *La Double Inconstance* is excused because the Prince is so attractive and Silvia comes to love him. Valville, In *La Vie de Marianne,* is forgiven for being overcome by the bosom of Mademoiselle Varthon; he is no different from other normal Frenchmen, we are told! Climal is a Tartuffe, but then he repents on his deathbed and leaves Marianne more than he was willing to pay for her surrender; in a similar way, Madame de Sainte-Hermières conspires with the abbé against Tervire but later repents; Marivaux could hardly believe that repentance undid past crimes, but it was not all to the good? Marianne, the virtuous orphan, the girl whom Madame de Miran defends in the name of "reason, humanity, and religion" (M, 328), knows her own ambiguity: "We are weak and do nasty things we do not wish to know about!" (M, 474).

Arlequin and other servants all too easily give in to their desires for food, drink, and money. As they rise in the scale of social responsibility, Marivaux' characters become more complex, more inextricably steeped in noble as well as evil motivations. Only once in a while there appears a clear-cut one-sided case like that of Frédéric in *Le Prince Travesti* or the scoundrels in *L'Héritier du Village* and *La Provinciale.* Most extreme perhaps is the ungrateful son who lets his mother starve; Tervire who finds her mother disconsolate and without means of support, violently upbraids her sister-in-law; the harshness of tone and the impotence of this protest may well be a major reason why Marivaux broke off *La Vie de Marianne* at this point. We gather that Tervire, bitter and frustrated, joined a convent but is none too sure she should advise Marianne to follow her in this decision. Violence does intrude into Marivaux' humane world and many times he felt Tervire's idealistic hate of those who render gentlemen impotent, unable to make their idea of justice triumph, but each time he caught himself and banished vituperation from his work, just as Classical tragedy excluded murder from the stage. For all that, evil does not disappear. Marivaux' image remains a realistic portrayal of the world torn between reason and unreason, ever intent to justify itself. All too often man believes in the illusion he is trying to create! The self-assured Jacob is one of the best examples. He does all he can to appear reasonable and virtuous. In this he is not unlike other characters: Is Dorante, in *Les Fausses Confidences,* not the successful lover because his repentance is so sincere, and in spite of all his schemes and tricks? Like Valville, or Jacob, he is no monster, just a man of his time, the most desirable known to Araminte! Such is Marivaux' realism, a moral realism that sees man very much as part of our world.

B. *Love and Sensibility*

Sensibility, as we have seen, was to be the link between author and reader, as stated in *Les Effets Surprenants*. Marivaux took it to be the distinguishing mark of true nobility, the quality which makes Silvia a worthy wife for the Prince in *La Double Inconstance,* the spirit that distinguishes Silvia and Dorante from their servants in *Le Jeu,* clearly perceptible even in their disguise. Marianne's noble sensibility enables her to rise in society even though she is a foundling. Even Jacob, her more daring masculine counterpart, is readily moved, and this is fortunate indeed: His generous rescues of Mademoiselle Habert on the Pont Neuf, and later, of a young nobleman fighting off assailants in the street, lead Jacob to his destiny, to comfort and wealth.

The principal theme, if not the only one, in Marivaux' work, is love and sensibility. Its relationships are modified by other passions, ambition, desire for power or rank, greed, all of which frequently outweigh the attractions of refinement and culture (cf. *Le Triomphe de Plutus*). Love must be distinguished from friendship since the eighteenth century saw the two concepts as fundamentally distinct and often not even complementary. Love is a violent passion, a fire that may quickly burn itself out, while friendship is an ideal, lasting relationship of two beings completely devoted to each other, a tie that rarely, if ever, rules the relationships between men and women, for it excludes desire and sensuality. Madame de Lambert, who stresses this point, speaks also for Marivaux. In *Les Effets,* Caliste extends hospitality and help to the less fortunate Clarice: This is friendship. Clorante, on the other hand, cannot help Clarice for he is ruled by his passion (love) for Caliste: This is how love destroys the very possibility of friendship. In *La Vie de Marianne,* the mutual devotion of the heroine and Madame de Miran is a supreme example of friendship, while Valville's passion for Marianne, and his subsequent passion for Mademoiselle Varthon, who makes him forget her, is a typical story of love, shifty and fickle: Valville is no monster (M, 375), for nature destines us for twenty loves rather than a single one (OD, 344) and love satisfied, without obstacles to overcome, is most likely to die (OD, 338). If infidelity were punished by death, men and women would fall by platoons (OD, 76). It is only natural to love those who are lovable (T I, 87).

Thus, friendship is a willful commitment; passion a force against which man is powerless; friendship is a utopian element in our world, love a driving force which affects most of our decisions. Marivaux was far more interested in its "surprising effects" than in dreams of perfection; we have pointed out how his allegorical plays, his island fantasies, or others set in some fairyland nonetheless are morally realistic, and portray men and women in all their ambiguity and complexity.

Examples abound. Gentlemen are fickle by nature, like Valville; women are "coquettes" who satisfy their vanity by taking lovers and use their intelligence to analyze where their heart has led them, to "catch up with their heart." Such is the central theme of the *Lettres Contenant une Aventure* and other early essays (OD). The plays and novels elaborate on the theme (cf. *La Dispute*). The knights of old, performing miracles of valor and constancy, and described in traditional novels, are eliminated by Marivaux, the resolute partisan of the Moderns. He realizes that "pleasure takes a powerful hold of the soul" *(tient furieusement à l'âme de l'homme, Télémaque,* OJ, 872), and let us note that he says, "the soul," and not just the body. Félicie, in the late play of that title, is dangerously given to pleasure and flirtation and is forced to admit that she is seeking everyone's love, not their friendship as she had believed, or pretended (T II, 742). She is in danger of turning into a Madame de Fécour, "more libertine than tender," offering love to all and friendship to none (P, 180). There are noble souls capable of true friendship, but Marivaux sets no superhuman standards; eternal love cannot be realized; the case of *La Femme Fidèle* is exceptional indeed and stands closer to traditional interpretations of Ulysses' return to Penelope than to the rest of Marivaux' work.

Love does encompass ideal aspects, tenderness for instance. Valville's tenderness makes him lovable (M, 66f, 74). However, an excess of tenderness becomes an unworldly "spirituality," a refinement of *préciosité* which Marivaux considers unrealistic or even contemptible. Apollo-Ergaste, in the *Triomphe de l'Amour,* is an eloquent example, and so is the need for the collaboration of Love with Cupid in *La Réunion des Amours.* This is what we called Marivaux' moral "realism."

For all of its inconstancy, the lack of assurance for the future, love provides the great moments in our lives, the unique experience that will affect our future attitudes. It may be true that "when one loves, reflection is powerless" (*Les Effets,* OJ, 199); the *Spectateur* introduces a girl undone by love (OD, 165); even so, the meeting of two hearts is infinitely significant; it is the unique moment, e.g., in *Le Jeu de l'Amour,* when Silvia "sees" her heart "with clearness" and avows that she has never experienced anything like it (T I, 829-31). In the *Surprise* of 1722, we hear of a "unique" encounter, a special experience *(une aventure singulière.* T I, 202, 234). In *Le Triomphe de l'Amour,* the protagonists are sure no one ever loved as much (T I, 945, cf. 844). This is the critical moment in Marivaux' works. Georges Poulet *(Etudes sur le Temps Humain)* derived his existentialist view of our author from this circumstance, but his formulation is too abstract, or rather reflects at best one aspect of Marivaux, who realized that there is something quite amusing when "unique moments" come to resemble each other: In *Les Serments Indiscrets,* Damis and Lucile speculate that their love ought to be unique, but there seem to be analogous cases elsewhere (T I, 993). This does not prevent them from surrendering to love, very much in spite of themselves, at the end of five long acts. The unique moment of love triumphs here as elsewhere. Nothing could be more absurd than to legislate against it, as the feminist leaders of *La Colonie* propose to do. Love pierces masks *(Le Jeu),* undoes solemn vows *(Les Serments),* upsets prejudice. Angélique tells Dorante, at the end of *Le Préjugé Vaincu:* "You have triumphed over my pride which I disavow, and my heart is there to avenge you" (T II, 667).

After such exultation, what of unfaithfulness? There is, indeed, little comfort in Marivaux' "happy endings," for they do not insure the future. It may be best not to speculate whether Dorante, in *Le Jeu de l'Amour,* will be able to keep his promise and never change. Who would bring up such a question in view of his immense happiness, a happiness he shares with Silvia?

Love and sensibility constitute the framework, the microcosm which lets Marivaux' characters perceive the problems of their lives, of society, of the world. If they lack love and sensibility, they turn into villains, seducers, perpetrators of violence; they unleash the forces of unreason. They are few in number and they do not often appear without redeeming features. Little can be said for Lelio in *La Fausse Suivante* or Frédéric in *Le Prince Travesti,* but the Prince in *La Double Inconstance* is lovingly tender and attractive, Dorante in *Les Fausses Confidences* is frank and sincere in his love, Lucidor, in *L'Epreuve,* will, supposedly, make a tender husband. Their faults will be forgotten more easily than the conceit that leads Madame Amelin to organize her entertainment at the expense of others *(Les Acteurs de Bonne Foi).* We might forgive Plutus in his "triumph" for he is more realistic than his opponent and hardly responsible for the fact others are money mad; we shall not admit as our friends those so easily corrupted by money, the scoundrels in *L'Héritier du Village*, in *La Provinciale*. Thus, love and sensibility are the requirement of appeal and virtue, but not accessible to everyone. The pretty dream of a world of sensibility, love, and polite speech does not dominate the creation of Marivaux. His is a more realistic perspective which validates his probing into man's duplicity.

C. *Sensuality*

This "realism" takes full account of man's sensuality. In *Pharsamon* we read that true passion is the very opposite of modern libertine attitudes (OJ, 510), but this applies only to ideal knights, to the dreamworld that is no more. Jacob may don the accoutrements of tradition and nobility, e.g., a sword, but his quest for success and love is undertaken in a different spirit! His wife-to-be is introduced as "a nymph of fifty" who advertises her well-preserved looks even while she denies doing so (P, 134, 103). The physical attributes of Mesdames Ferval and Fécour are prominently displayed (P, 142, 170). Jacob and Mademoiselle Habert are advised there is nothing like being man and wife for making love (P, 100) and their bedroom scenes are hilarious, almost grotesque: "What a pleasure to frustrate the rights of the devil and, without sin, be as satisfied as are sinners" (P, 163, 189). Sensuality is taken to be part of life. Cupid demands a "fitting respect for what sustains the world" (T I, 871).

"Vice" and eroticism are, however, rejected; it may have its "brutish satisfactions, but it not only kills love, should there be any, it does not even appeal as much as tender, innocent love" (OD, 206-7). Marianne agrees: "A woman who offends decency loses all the attractions of her charms" (M, 208). There is an almost puritan side to Marivaux, when he protests against the negligee, society's excuse for public nudity (OD, 28, T I, 493-94), or when he has an army officer reprimand a young author, who represents Crébillon fils, for cheap eroticism (P, 200-201). Sensuality is everpresent, but it is acceptable only as part of a loving relationship. As Marianne puts it: "In love, we very delicately perform some very indelicate acts . . . . The man who wants you more than he loves you, is an evil suitor" (M, 40-41).

Of course, such a rule is not always observed; it is a moral objective. In *Pharsamon* we read that often lovers overlook certain formalities (OJ, 464), e.g., the marriage ceremony which, in *L'Ile de la Raison*, are said to be unnecessary to the wise (T I, 648). The danger arises when impetuous passion does not worry about love. In *L'Amour et la Vérité* we read: "Most lovers owe their success to moments like these" (T I, 64). The desires of the Fairy Queen in *Arlequin Poli par l'Amour* appear as ugly as she. *Le Cabinet du Philosophe* expands on Marianne's explanations: "Women would blush at the kind of 'respect' we have for them!" The "brutal" invitation: "Madame, I desire you very much, . . . please grant me your favors!" is not different in meaning from the delicate declaration: "I love you, you have a thousand charms in my eyes" (OD, 637-39).

Paul Gazagne concluded that when Marivaux says "love," he means "seduction," when he refers to inclination he means desire *(Marivaux par Lui-Même)*, but this is going too far, just as when Planchon staged *La Seconde Surprise de l'Amour* with an imposing bed, first well made-up, later rumpled (T I, 664), but the implication of sensuality is everpresent in Marivaux who mocks the pedantic advice of a Hortensius; philosophy is unsuited to counter the dangers of love! Plutus wins out over Apollo in *Le Triomphe de Plutus,* Léonide in her multiple disguises outwits both Hermocrate and Léontine in *Le Triomphe de l'Amour.* The life force carries the day; it is stronger than philosophy, more powerful than convention. Nature needs life even more than love (P, 230). The young girl in *La Voiture Embourbée* who tells of infidelity on the farm sets the tone of realism and, to Marivaux as well as to the reader, appears more natural and acceptable than the would-be wit and her romantic mother, steeped in tales of oriental horror. Marivaux rejects such figments as aberrations of literature, useless and unreal. In this connection, the term "literature" can be interpreted as later by Rousseau when he rejected its fancies in favor of the truth (in his *Confessions*).

While outdated sentimentality is rejected in favor of the forces of life, the need for sentiment is reaffirmed. "The reason of the heart" is a concept that links Marivaux and Rousseau. It involves the restraints reason imposes on human nature, etiquette, the code of the gentleman, sociability, the ethics of humanism. However, the problems involved can be assessed only if all of human nature is taken into account, including sensuality.

On the Island of Reason, marriage is quickly arranged but only under the rule of reason, i.e., when everyone understands the needs of others. A Frédéric Deloffre points out, this is no sanction of free love but a plea for a more natural society, a less legalistic view of marriage contracts.

The role of sensuality in Marivaux' work bears out his realism. He does not retreat from the marketplace. "Marivaudage" designates the play with contrasting meanings and motives, but it is no abstraction as many critics used to believe. Marivaux viewed life, all of it.

D. Honnêteté, *the Ethics of the Gentleman*

The contradictory meanings of the terms, *honnête, honnête homme, honnêteté,* are an excellent illustration of the point. They illustrate the ambiguity of those who would be gentlemen. The ideal itself is rarely encountered. When Marivaux' characters proclaim they are gentlemen, they state a wish or an opinion, a sham, a delusion; they do not become gentlemen by claiming such distinction! They are real in their hopes and fears; there are no shining knights in armor!

Marivaux plays with the meanings of *honnête* such as we might find them defined by Littré, "polite, of good upbringing, appealing, conforming to etiquette, sensitive, frank, honest, honorable." These meanings are further multiplied by the comic and paradoxical circumstances to which they apply. In satiricial context, they will designate the shortcomings of would-be gentlemen or of those derelict in their duties, for, in the eyes of Marivaux, gentlemen have duties; privilege imposes obligations, but then even gentlemen are human!

It is essential to observe that the ideal of the gentleman was derived from that of the courtier and, originally, applied only to nobility. Marivaux applies the term to the standards of behavior of everyone with due respect for their concerns and motivations. The wealthy and the poor, the masters and the servants will see their functions from their peculiar point of view. Examples abound. We shall have to limit ourselves to a few illustrations for each of five basic meanings of *honnête.*[1]

(1) *Polite.* Gentlemen are polite and "politeness offends no one," as we read in the *Indigent Philosophe* (OD, 322), but there are problems: Geneviève is polite but, hélas, this is not sufficient virtue to make her a fitting wife for Jacob (P, 27-29). The Prince in *La Double Inconstance* is a model of politeness, but for all that he can be accused of seduction (or even rape). And what of gentlemen who turn out to be boors without sufficient respect for their inferiors whom they call "Hé!" as in *L'Ile des Esclaves?* On the Island of Reason it is the Countess, the Courtier, the masters altogether, who have the greatest difficulty becoming considerate (polite), as they must, to become great (and tall), while Blaise and Lisette, ever so much less trained in the ways of society, succeed rapidly.

Politeness which is mere conformity with etiquette is not enough to make a gentleman. Climal, the seducer, prides himself on being polite, but this makes him no less detestable. We are reminded of Pyrrhus, in Racine's *Andromaque,* who addresses the heroine as "Madame" just before threatening to kill her son unless she surrender to him. Polite language scarcely compensates for ugly passions and these destroy our idea of the gentleman.

(2) *Trustworthy.* By definition, a gentleman can be trusted, but in the *Spectateur* a girl is undone because she trusted appearances! (OD, 155). Spinette voices grave doubts about Plutus and his wealth, for she wants to safeguard her virtue (T I, 742). Marianne would have us believe that she considered Climal trustworthy—until it was almost too late; but then, as Father Saint-Vincent puts it, if one cannot trust a man so respected by society, whom shall we trust? (M, 143). We conclude that true gentlemen are rare indeed, and generally less successful than Plutus and Climal!

(3) *Appealing.* A gentleman is expected to appeal through his looks as well as his character; he will be well dressed and well mannered. Here again there is danger, for we may be taken in by the glitter of false virtue. One episode in *La Fausse Suivante* is like a pun on these contrasts. Lelio, who intends to marry for money, faces Trivelin who is no more of a gentleman than he. Suddenly Lelio pulls his sword. "You would scare me, except for your air of a gentleman," says Trivelin (T I, 454). Are we to assume that if Lelio looked like the scoundrel he was he would have been more dangerous? Or that the looks of a gentleman are always reassuring? In any event, Trivelin is right for Lelio does not strike him; he was disarmed by the term, "gentleman."

In one of the first scenes of *Le Jeu,* Silvia protests that she will not hear of Dorante, but Lisette comforts her: She has heard that Dorante looks every inch like a gentleman (T I, 800). Appealing looks provoke love on first sight, in the *Jeu* as in the early novels and in other plays (T I, 501, 896). But "can a rascal not look like a gentleman?" (P, 63). Ironically, the question is put by a most unappealing character, the confessor of the Habert sisters, outraged that the younger one "fell" for Jacob, and he is right for Jacob does not qualify as a gentleman; but then neither does he, nor the Fairy Queen in *Arlequin Poli* who considers herself so attractive and entitled to Arlequin's love, nor Climal intent on seducing Marianne but anxious to maintain the airs of a gentleman (M, 119). If, as Marianne says, virtue is always appealing (M, 337), must we conclude that all who appeal are virtuous? Marianne herself is ambivalent; she makes the most of her charms and pretense of virtue to rise in society. Marivaux plays not only with contrasts between true qualities and outer appearances, but between degrees of deceit and delusion.

(4) *Frank, sincere.* Gentlemen should be sincere; Marivaux' work can be interpreted as a constant search for sincerity, but he plays with the term as with all others. Jacob is frank indeed when he proclaims that he cannot stand feminine modesty (P, 140). He is disarmingly forthright, never hides that he is attracted by ladies, but what shall we say when he takes on the title of nobility as Monsieur de la Vallée or when he starts hiding his peasant origins and says he is born of "honest folk" (P, 133), a pun indeed, for the French term *(honnêtes gens)* also means "gentlemen." Jacob is a disquieting mixture of forthrightness and self-interest. He accepts Geneviève's money but not her hand in marriage and claims superior virtue that is not his; but then he accepts not only the title of nobility but its obligations when he defends a young nobleman and saves his life.

Sincerity is a virtue, but *Les Sincères,* the Marquise and Ergaste who make a fetish of it, are repelled by each other and driven back into the arms of partners who show understanding and admiration. Sincerity is the principle that guides Marivaux' search for the truth, in analyzing character, but is he not also the author who spoke least of himself and made it difficult to constitute his biography? The sincerity of Dorante, in *Les Fausses Confidences,* is what makes Araminte forgive all his tricks, his lies which were all but frank and sincere. Who, then, is a gentleman? Would Marivaux claim to possess the required sincerity? He would ask our indulgence for being as human as the gentlemen he depicts, though there is no evidence that he possessed their foibles. Ultimately his ideal of the gentleman implies a fundamental humanism and understanding, the "reason of the heart."

(5) *Honorable.* Being honorable, says Arlequin, "is my only claim to fame," as he tries to get Frédéric to call him *Monseigneur* in exchange for not so honorable services (T I, 357). Similarly, Trivelin bravely calls himself a gentleman even though he admits that his actions are honorable only when need be (T I, 412, 434). No gentleman would inflict himself on a girl, and this is the maxim quoted by Angélique to persuade Frontin to leave her, as he does, even though he is no gentleman, but a servant of Lucidor sent to test her (T II, 536).

These examples pertain to members of the servant class who pretend to high principles which cannot guide them, even when they are disguised like Arlequin in the *Jeu.* However, if we examine Marianne, whose noble origins are attested by the presence of servants when her parents were killed. Marianne, who insists on being honorable and who appeals because she clings to the path of virtue, we find her morality too flexible to be truly "honorable" (M, 48). She has our sympathy in making her presence accepted in society, but how haughtily she rejects Villot, whose humble origins and modest intellect repel her; ironically Villot is introduced as an *"honnête homme"* (M, 308, 311, 317, 332), an "honorable" fellow who happens to be no match for her.

In some of the late essays and allocutions, where Marivaux speaks without humorous and paradoxical intent, he shows that he holds firmly to the ideal of honor. He explains that the true gentleman will be proud and honorable, that he will be the one to state his opinions frankly and not hide facts to flatter his prince (OD, 521). Such a declaration comes as no surprise, for the ideal of honor is always clearly implied, especially in the heroic comedies like *Le Prince Travesti*, where kings in disguise can be recognized by their sterling qualities; in *Le Triomphe de l'Amour*, another heroic comedy, only pedants like Hermocrate and Léontine are deceived; Agis senses the honorable design of Léonide-Phocion as soon as he sees her (him); the confusion of sexes is characteristic of the ambiguity of situations and personalities, but leaves the ideal untarnished. After all, an honorable, sensitive, gentlemanly character, like that of Dorante and Silvia in *Le Jeu,* easily and clearly shines through all disguises.

We conclude that Marivaux is an idealist, a humanist, but no easy optimist. He portrays ever so many would-be gentlemen who can do no more than pretend to act the part: Plutus, Climal, Jacob, Trivelin. Were they truly frank, they would speak like the characters in the "True World" of the *Cabinet du Philosophe* (and at times, Plutus and Jacob comes close to doing so), but let us recall that the Paris there described is more sincere, but not more honorable than reality. Disreputable designs, e.g., on an inheritance, are merely made more evident.

Everywhere Marivaux sees pretense and dissimulation; even in moments when he pictures himself as a compassionate "spectator" coming to the aid of a defenseless girl or protesting against overbearing power (OD, 129, 131-32, 135, etc.) or when he proposes a model for the education of a prince, he does not show honor triumphant. The concept of the gentleman remains an ideal, a guiding principle in a world beset by ambivalence and the inability to attain it. The persistent use of *honnête* and terms related indicates Marivaux' concern. He is a pragmatic humorist who maintains a moral view of the world.

E. *Vanity, Man's Second Nature*

"Self-love is to the human mind what form is to matter" (OD, 35). Women flirt (OD, 76, 371f) while men play with good manners as with a hobbyhorse (OD, 380). "I don't want to be a coquette," says Lucile in *Les Serments Indiscrets,* "but there are times when your heart impels you that way and when it feels good to have eyes that are free to roam in all directions" (T I, 971). She sets her pride on preserving this freedom and suffers through five acts, resisting the urge to marry. Even so, she wants to attract Damis. Similarly, Silvia, in the *Jeu,* sets her "insatiable" vanity on getting Dorante to declare himself even though he believes that she is a servant girl.

Marianne's vanity has been singled out as a dominant force by critics like Ruth Jamieson and Lester Crocker.[2] She is as intent on success as Jacob, be it through her looks (M, 49-50) or be renouncing the right to marry Valville, to obtain him more readily. She displays her charms in church (M, 52-62) not unlike women sporting negligees (OD, 28) or the Countess in *L'Ile de la Raison* who devotes hours to the "architecture" of her hair, her ribbons, and sweet looks, all carefully practiced (T I, 627-28).

Vanity produces ostentation of wealth in expensive clothes, public ceremony, or pomp; it inflicts charity while wounding the recipient's pride. Marivaux protests against it in the *Spectateur* (no. 5-6); such display irks him even more than the vanity of coquettes, a theme to which he returns frequently. "Our coquetry is simply prodigious," says one of the women in *La Colonie* (T II, 687, cf. 96), but the urge to please is not confined to women. The Poet in *L'Ile de la Raison* writes to be praised; "praise is a lovely thing" (T I, 611). The *Cabinet du Philosophe* speaks of the pleasing sensation of being known as a gentleman.

The ideal of the gentleman could be a positive, moral force, but vanity perverts it; it subordinates it to the individual will, to man's self-centered desires. Marivaux follows La Rochefoucauld; he is no convert to the philosophy of enlightened self-interest as we later find it in Helvétius. Marianne's renunciation of Valville may suggest such a view, for she proposes sacrifices for greater gains in the end, but she had no way to foresee them. If the noble actions of Marianne and Jacob are generously rewarded, the author's intent is irony.

Closely related are the descriptions of the desire for respectability, but also power and influence, due to vanity. Many characters parade as gentlemen only to attain their goals; they may also be in love out of vanity, like the fops in *Le Petit-Maître Corrigé*. Marivaux relates almost every manifestation of the will, or vanity, to the theme of love and often love must triumph over vanity, as it does in *Le Préjugé Vaincu*.

Vanity rules even in *La Dispute* where both sexes are observed in their "natural" state. They are found to fall in love, separate, or be faithful like their counterparts in society. Eglé is first enraptured by her mirror-image (T II, 605), then lets herself be loved only to "fall" for another man. Vanity causes two couples to switch partners because they are so proud to capture new love. The self is dominant all too often. Marivaux states several times that it is the selfless who suffer.

F. *Society and Status*

These views suggest that the social context, the desire for social success, and vanity activate all of our actions. Man appears as the tool of his desires. The Philosopher on the Island of Reason seeks to dominate by the use and abuse of logic. Frédéric, in *Le Prince Travesti*, deals in power and influence. The Prince, in *La Double Inconstance*, can be accused of seducing Silvia even though she falls in love with him without knowing he is the one who planned her surrender and organized the defection of Arlequin. Are these characters worse than Marianne and Jacob who use every means at their disposal to further their ambitions? The parallel fate of Marivaux' characters in their quest to succeed indicates that he pursues universals, though in individual dress. The need for recognition beckons to all.

This drive affects masters and servants in very different ways. Their criteria for judging success are not the same. The servants are most concerned with food, drink, and money, the means to acquire them. Arlequin, in *La Double Inconstance*, lets himself be tempted by a wonderful meal, the obstacle placed in his path by the Prince who wants to separate him from Silvia. She is more refined and bitterly resents being put off for food and drink (T I, 295). Lépine, the scoundrel and mastermind in *Le Legs*, mockingly speaks of the servant mentality of Lisette. Servants are creatures who crawl like ants! (T II, 332). Lépine better beware, for his status is no loftier than hers and soon he will marry her!

The clearest contrast between the sensitivity of masters and servants is presented in *Le Jeu de l'Amour*. The noble feelings of Dorante and Silvia find their parody in Arlequin and Lisette; here we have an example of that rare species, the true gentleman or lady, whose refinement is inborn, while the servants are at best mirror images of their superiors, distorted reflections even while emulating them. The contrast introduces opposing social levels with corresponding levels of understanding. The parallel leads to a double marriage, but servants will never be masters! At best they may conspire to prevent their masters' marriage, as in *Les Sincères*, or motivate it, as in *Le Préjugé Vaincu;* there Lisette requires that Angélique marry before she, Lisette, will follow Angélique's advice and do so herself (T II, 662f).

Social success, money, influence, and power thus affect masters and servants, the latter in a more naïve, often grotesque frame of reference. The servants are less afflicted by social convention, less deeply corrupted than their superiors and, therefore, more readily reformed in the island plays.

Similar parallels can be established between men and women, equally affected by corruption even though women are called the weaker sex (T I, 466, 523). They become more readily the toys of their own vanity, but they are no more inclined to vice than men. There is agreement concerning this in *La Dispute* (T II, 603f). The fundamental problem is one each individual must face when he is tempted; he must decide whether to yield to temptation, dominate others, seek personal gain, or remain true to himself. The choice is rarely a simple matter.

One form of overbearing is particularly offensive to Marivaux, the abuse of charity, the tendency of the wealthy to make others feel their inferiority. As one who suffered because of his limited means, he was proud enough not to want to depend on others. There are a number of such passages in the *Spectateur,* written when Marivaux suffered major losses (OD, 129-31, 180f, 266), others in the *Cabinet du Philosophe* (OD, 361) and in *La Vie de Marianne.* The heroine castigates "charity that has no shame" and serves only the glory of those who perpetrate it (M, 29-30), but she is not immune to the lure of society and privilege. She succumbs to pride herself when Madame Dutour reveals her origins (M, 262-63). Marianne is too intent on advancing herself to accept the intrusions of Madame Dutour and of the humble Villot who is proposed as a husband. All this shows that greater dangers threaten our modesty as we attain status and wealth; however, Marivaux does not idealize poverty. He paints a harsh picture of the lower classes (OD, 10-14) and shows that relying on charity is torture.

There is movement in different social classes. If Marianne and Jacob rise, as do Silvia in *La Double Inconstance* and Dorante in *Les Fausses Confidences* and *Le Préjugé Vaincu,* other characters value love more than rank and marry below their status. Rank, or wealth, may be acquired, lost, or overlooked, as the case may be. Often, social conditions are central to the action of a play. They emphasize what we have called Marivaux' realism. The money question is spelled out in remarkable detail in such plays as *La Fausse Suivante, L'Héritier du Village, Le Triomphe de Plutus, Le Chemin de la Fortune, Le Legs, Les Fausses Confidences, La Provinciale.* Money will serve even the *Indigent Philosophe* as he prefers "ruinous follies" to the "sad follies" of the poor (OD, 280); he sees nothing desirable in drinking water as long as wine is available. Austerity appeals no more to him than to Marivaux, the Epicurean. The term must be understood. Marivaux speaks of the thrill *(volupté)* of doing good (OD, 132); he does not confine the Epicurean ideal to any one class. Indeed, the "philosophical bum" may achieve happiness in life more easily than kings or aristocrats.

Status does not confer merit. The noblemen in *L'Héritier du Village* are crooks. In *Le Préjugé Vaincu* we read: "A princess may well have been badly brought up" (T II, 644). Arléquin is often no better; he makes up for his deficiencies by good will. The masses may be more like wild animals, stormy, rash, childlike in behavior, while noblemen may have no distinction but their title; the wealthy may make their power a burden to others.

Thus Marivaux' canvas of society is more inclusive than has often been assumed. It encompasses princes and slaves (those working in the mines in *Les Effets*), it includes noblemen, the bourgeois, priests, peasants, servants, also soldiers and the cruelty of war (*Télémaque Travesti;* also the *Homère Travesti*). The implications may be revolutionary, but not the intent, for the human problem, the individual, retains primary significance. Man is presented in his social context. It presents him with temptations but, above all, with amusing quandaries: "The differences in social conditions are a test of God" (OD, 542).

This raises the fundamental question of evil. Marivaux describes Paris as a school for evil where vices are far more in evidence than virtues; man's potential for either good or evil is in great danger there (OD, 9-10). This view of 1717 is not fundamentally different from that expressed in *Le Cabinet du Philosophe* (*Le Monde Vrai,* 1734) or in the *Paysan Parvenu.* When Jacob arrives in Paris, "he has not had time to be corrupted" (P, 43), but soon thereafter we find him "lost in vanity," the gay and sociable kind which, for all its amusing exterior, is no less a school for luxury and perversion: "As the soul becomes refined, it is corrupted" (P, 187).

Here Marivaux anticipates Rousseau. Indeed, he moves closer to his views; first he shows man born evil, forced to fight his weaknesses like a monster (OD, 234), while, in 1755, he speaks of man as born innocent and insists on his capacity to develop or pervert his personality. Vanity is all-important; man is ruled by his desire for social success. Were mathematics required for social advancement, no one would ever claim to be incapable of mastering the subject (OD, 483-90). Marivaux lacks Rousseau's polemical purpose, but he sets the stage for his radical opposition to the idea of original sin. Of course, he remains the author of comedy; he emphasizes the amusing ambiguity of man's motives, not perdition; he stays in the society he loves rather than fleeing it. Rousseau is ever so much closer to Molière's Alceste set to embark for a desert island.[3]

G. *Religion, Ethics, and the Progress of Man*

Marivaux focuses his attention on the worldly society of which he is a part, but he is concerned with religious issues. Tervire's advice to Marianne in the last three parts of the novel is significant: Marianne should not leave "the world" unless she feels a compelling need. The entry of Marivaux' daughter into a convent, a few years after he wrote these sections, must have been hard for him to accept. However, he stands closer to religion than most contemporary authors. He advises: "In matters of religion . . . argue only with the heart," and goes on to emphasize mystery (OD, 353-54). He explains that half of religion consists of the mysteries man is to believe, the other half of self-sacrifice; its demands are analogous to those of the ruler who asks us to forego some of our freedom for the sake of good government (OD, 342). He affirms that he stands by the side of religion (OD, 217, 281) and speaks out against atheists who "brazenly walk in darkness," replacing our perennial philosophy with a few libertine ideas (OD, 197). There are those with the unfortunate courage to live without faith (OD, 426f) and deists[4] who take themselves to be the judges of all things and thus corrupt human judgment (OD, 419).

These passages from Marivaux' periodicals transcend his usual tone of humorous analysis. Others, more numerous, maintain the comic vein, and identify pretense and hypocrisy. They imply the failure of the Church as an institution. The gallery of its inadequate representatives looms large in Marivaux' work. The country priest in *La Voiture Embourbée* is a hard man, difficult to persuade to take in the stranded travellers. His son, who adds a platitudinous conclusion to the story they invent to entertain themselves, proves that there is little intelligence to be derived from his milieu. We find other caricatures of men of religion, such as the curé in the *Télémaque Travesti* (OJ, 753) and Father Saint-Vincent in *La Vie de Marianne* who delivers the heroine right into the clutches of her seducer, Climal. The naïveté of Father Saint-Vincent can hardly be surpassed; he will not believe the truth even when it has become abundantly clear. "If you are right," he confesses to Marianne, "whom can we trust?" (M, 137-43). Climal, a worthy successor to Tartuffe, may be unmasked (M, 108-13), but he continues to declare his love for her (M, 187) and does not repent until he dies (M, 246-49); he even leaves Marianne more money than he had been willing to pay her as his mistress. Father Saint-Vincent may consider that thus religion triumphs after all, but the reader smiles at his simplicity of mind!

A parallel scene of repentance is that of Madame de Sainte-Hermières in the same novel. She had first conspired to place Tervire in a convent as a way to rid herself of her charge, than to marry her off to Sercour, then to ruin her reputation through a plot with Sercour's nephew, the abbé, a villain within the church! Again the truth wins out on a deathbed, but this is little comfort (M, 454f, 481f).

In the *Paysan Parvenu,* the confessor of the Habert sisters is as intent on his power over them as the abbé was on inheriting the fortune of his uncle. This confessor is a tyrant who quotes the Bible only to suit his purposes (P, 42, 58-65, esp. 63). The older sister is a typical *dévote* who replaces the pleasure of sinning by the thrill of discovering sin in others (P, 47-50), and who takes her hatred of you as proof that you are worth nothing (P, 161, cf. 227). Such narrow-minded piety destroys the happiness of others. It is the very antithesis of self-sacrifice and service which are essential aspects of true religion and, for that matter, of reason as understood in *L'Ile de la Raison.*

Inhumanity perpetrated in the name of religion is a major theme in the *Télémaque Travesti;* the persecution of the Huguenots and the horrors of the Camisard wars are vividly described (OJ, 832-51, 844-900). We recall the grotesque peace arranged by the hero and his mentor; it will protect the Protestant peasants at least from the abduction of their daughters. Religion is all too often abused or taken in vain. Marivaux protests against the methods of the confessor in the *Paysan Parvenu* with a typical understatement: "The Bible cannot be used to justify all of man's strange fantasies" (P 68). It is significant that his religious satire is confined to the novels. Marivaux created a

Tartuffe in Climal, but he never placed such a figure on the stage! He avoided the scandal of confrontation.

A man like the Archbishop of Sens, dedicated to the idea that morality is inculcated through religious argument and that literature, if it should fail to do so, is pernicious, could hardly agree with Marivaux' presentation of man's ambiguity and, in particular, of the inadequacy of men of the Church. As a result, the Archbishop honored Marivaux with the most unusual and negative welcome to the French Academy, extending greetings only to the gentleman, not to the author. Of course, the Archbishop lacked literary appreciation; he misunderstood the grand tradition of French Classicism; above all, he failed to realize that Marivaux could be his ally through his religious temperament and his desire to "reason" with the emotions. After all, it was the appeal to emotion and sensitivity that was to transform religious thought in France from Rousseau to Chateaubriand! (Cf. section F above on Marivaux and Rousseau).

It would be misleading to present Marivaux' ethics only in religious terms. If preaching, or teaching of principles is ineffective, the very framework of organized religion could easily become superfluous. *Philosophes* like Voltaire or Diderot believed at least in the usefulness of religion for controlling the masses; Marivaux is not even sure of that. He pictures the lower classes *(le peuple)* of Paris as inaccessible to religion, in heart and mind. They may be swayed by a loudmouthed preacher, but no moral lesson will penetrate (OD, 13).

Still the ethical problem remains. Good and evil are the poles that encompass life; they provide a scale for measuring our actions. Interestingly, Marivaux concentrates not on the two principles, or absolutes, but on what lies in between. In the *Lettres sur les Habitants de Paris* of 1717, Marivaux identifies three groups of citizens: Those who succumb to evil abound in all walks of life; "the just" represent a small elite; then there is the all-important third group of gentlemen citizens *(honnêtes gens)* who practice as much good as etiquette requires, for they aim to satisfy convention (OD, 9). As Plutus says: "There is nothing as beautiful as propriety" *(les bienséances,* T I, 755). In the *Paysan* we find many characters who belong in this third group, e.g., Madame de Ferval who lives "in the honorable state of being looked upon as good; this prevents her from seeming evil even while she foments malice all about her; she just does not realize how evil she is" (P, 143).

Clearly, no moral society can be established on such an attitude but, precisely, Marivaux never assumes that the ideal can be realized. Above all, he knows that he could not bring it about by didactic writing and moral protest. He supposes that his reader, or spectator, will be like Angélique in *L'Ecole des Mères,* "naturally virtuous," but apt to go to sleep when confronted with sermons on good behavior (T II, 22). Angélique is convinced that her mother is ill-advised to lecture to her, especially since she does not touch on the experience of life and, worse yet, would force on her a frustrating marriage to an old man (T II, 18, 21). Elsewhere, Marivaux repeats: Sermons on vanity are lifeless, mere "spirituality" (OD, 357).

What, then, is an author to do? First, become a *moraliste* who analyzes and amuses, rather than a moralist who teaches like any pretentious pedant; second, imply as much of his humanism as can be reconciled with the requirements of literature. As stated in *La Voiture Embourbée,* "nothing that might inspire virtue should be considered foolish" (OJ, 354). Virtue can be shown to be attractive while the ugliness of vice can be made manifest (OD, 132, 217). What if such an image does not conform to reality? "I may be wrong, but it will all be for the good of morals" (OD, 260). Here he comes close to an intransigent idealism, but it is a passing mood. Marivaux asserts that the true gentleman, would never reply in kind to offenses (*lâchetés,* T I, 374) even though this leaves him defenseless and even ineffective: "The true gentleman is the person you always want to deal with, although you do not wish to be like him" (OD, 309). As Marianne notes, the virtuous suffer constantly (M, 18); even so, our author maintains, "a virtuous man is not a fool!" (OD, 305-6).

Once again we catch him in one of those rare moments when he speaks his mind without letting humor, irony, or fantasy intervene in the account. He feels a kind of outrage that most crime goes unpunished, that many guilty persons are held in high honor (OD, 362), that punishment administered by the courts is often cruel, a "remedy" far worse than the ills it is to cure. His sympathy is with the poor, even when they commit desperate acts (OD, 363) for "human malice is rich" (OD, 370).

More commonly, he sees the world like Jacob who says that we all have our faults, tend to sin, wish to camouflage our unworthiness (P, 49, 64, 68); Marivaux tends to excuse Marianne's scheming, her apparent virtue that wins over the Minister in charge of the hostile family council who concludes: "Can we stop virtue from pleasing?" (M, 337). He was, of course, not won over by pure virtue but then, as Marivaux repeats from his earliest preface to his late comments on style, the truth is communicated through the heart (D, 364). Marianne knows how to appeal to it; is she not better than most of those she must convince of her worth?

The emphasis remains on ambiguity. Marivaux presents his dubious situations and even fundamental issues of ethics in humorous terms; he makes us smile at the shortcomings of the Church, at human weaknesses, and selfish motives; he hides his indignation which breaks through only here and there in his periodicals and essays.

In view of this moral realism, his often pessimistic appraisal of man, how then could he believe in progress? For he does. He is convinced of the continuous expansion of knowledge and culture, the immense superiority of modern writers over those of antiquity. He expresses this in his early diatribes against Homer (*Télémaque Travesti,* OJ, 718f, *Homère Travesti, Spectateur,* OD, 159, etc.), in his open support for the Moderns (OD, 144, 148, 176, *La Fausse Suivante* T I, 413-14), in his attacks against pedants like Hortensius who think that sterile wisdom can defeat love (*La Seconde Surprise,* T I, 697), and other passages culminating in *Le Miroir* of 1755, where he repeats that the human spirit keeps moving forward, that never before have there been so many men of genius (OD, 456-57). His only concession: Insights can be forgotten, the accrued wealth of ideas misused, taste can be lost (OD, 459). Even so, he remains convinced that the modern potential is infinitely greater than that of the past. His faith in progress is unimpaired.

It must be understood that the party position of the Moderns was adopted by him as a significant protest against authority, the supposed authority of the Ancients whose model was used to justify outdated methods of instruction in the schools, standards of style and rhetoric not germane to the purposes of a creative mind, also inordinate criticism of his own writing. Marivaux felt that such opinions were emitted by second-rate minds who shielded their ineptitude behind the glory of antiquity.

The Moderns were associated in his mind with the new forms of analysis he inherited from Malebranche, the new critical spirit of Fontenelle, the intellectual milieu of Madame de Lambert. There resulted a long-standing allegiance to the idea of progress, a philosophic optimism that sees "man as a being in chains who seeks to break his shackles" (OD, 353) and believes that gradually man is doing so. This guiding ideal is in no way circumscribed by the fallible nature of man, his ambiguity, his self-centered motives, his use of moral precept for selfish purposes. A pragmatic realism and a good sense of humor moderates, but does not limit the underlying optimism of Marivaux.

He believes in the progressive expansion of reason. The way he defines it, this includes the requirement of humility and service to others which is also "half" of religion. Thus rationalism and faith coincide: the ethical ideal approximates the religious one. Categorical divisions of the thought of his day into rationalist and religious camps are illusory, at best gross simplifications inappropriate to the comprehension of Marivaux.

All too long critics have held that a comic author is no philosopher, that *marivaudage* precludes fundamental insight, that his play on feelings and motives is merely amusing, never profound. We hope that we have countered these charges. Marivaux' humanistic ideal, implied rather than explicated, appears clear and challenging. His intelligent analysis of man's ambiguity is a relevent commentary, not in spite of the fact, but because it is amusing and suggestive.

CHAPTER 8

Conclusion

IN his preface to the *Homère Travesti,* and several times thereafter, Marivaux stated that our appreciation quickly tires. We become satiated and require the new! This was part of his polemics against the adulation of the Classics, a defense of his originality. Would he not be surprised to find himself, today, one of these "Classics," with devotees attending his plays, rereading his novels and essays; scholars surveying every conceivable document that might throw light on his background and family, on personal matters he carefully tried to hide from the public eye; professors, students writing weighty dissertations where he made fun of an erudition he could not have imagined devoted to modern literature! Of course, Classics no longer deprive contemporary authors of their livelihood, of their right to be heard or performed, but Marivaux asserted, in fact, that it is human nature to prefer the latest productions. The argument could be turned against him; it does not apply! His works are again in print, performances about equal those of Molière, the modern temperament has found in him themes akin to its own. What we need is more, and more adequate translations!

The variety of his styles is outstanding, adapted as they are to the individuality of his characters. His art of dialogue attracts us, his intellectual humor playing with meanings and implications, his approach to the truth on several levels, the broad scope of his work. He was, of course, a man of his time. His milieu militated against rollicking realism like that of his early parodies; it also made him formulate his observations in the framework of salon society, so that most passions and emotions are related to love—as they are on the French Classical stage—and that the focus is on the individual, even though he does appear in his social context; we have found commentary on classes, money matters, conditions in Paris, but these are mostly incidental. All this indicates that he adapted to the circumstances under which he had to work, e.g., the capacities of the actors of the Italian troupe. The adaption of Racine and Marivaux to the requirements of the stage is one of their notable accomplishments. Their originality starts there. Marivaux was fascinated with words, with ideas; he was a brilliant conversationalist as we know, e.g., from the abbé Trublet; he said a great deal about man, his motives, quandaries, and illusions, and expressed these in the most amusing way possible. He laid down his pen when he had had his say; he left novels incomplete rather than adding obvious sequels. This too is greatly to his credit.

His objective was to shed light on his characters, just the sufficient amount to be pertinent and suggestive. From this twilight atmosphere (Suzanne Mühlemann speaks of the *clair-obscur* in *Ombres et Lumières dans . . . Marivaux*) comes knowledge of the self, the "science of the human heart" which he described before the French Academy. He set out to create comedy with meaning and intellectual content, an analysis of emotions that are significant. In this, we believe, Marivaux has succeeded. We hope our readers will share our enthusiasm.

Notes and References

Chapter Three

1. For the *Lettre a une Dame sur la Perte d'un Perroquet* of 1718, see the discussion of *Bilboquet* (above).

2. Ed. Rodis-Lewis (Paris, 1962) I, 4, 150; II, 27, for this and the following references.

Chapter Four

1. A second tragedy, *Mahomet Second,* remained incomplete; the fragment will be included in a new edition of the *Théâtre Complet* (ed. Deloffre). Written about 1726, when Voltaire argued with La Motte over the need for verse in tragedy, the fragment first appeared in the *Mercure* of March, 1747. It was discovered by Henri Lagrave.

2. *Traité de l'Amitié* in *Oeuvres* I, 435.

3. *Nivelle de la Chaussee* (Paris, 1887), pp. 67-68. There are instances in the repertoire of the old Italian troupe, in the theater of Regnard and Dufresny (cf. T I, 397-98), also in Book 4, Chs. 4-5 of *Gil Blas* by Lesage (1724), where Aurore de Guzman is disguised as Félix de Mendoce.

4. In the *Lettres sur les Habitants de Paris,* the negligee is called a subterfuge for nudity (OD 28); in *Le Dénouement Imprévu,* Mademoiselle Argante would wear a negligee to reveal herself to Eraste, just to convince her father she is mad: "So that he will see only me and that will be all to the good" (T I, 494).

5. The name, Blectrue, seems to stem from *blictri,* taken to mean a rational idea of God by John Toland; this shows the influence of deism on Marivaux. Cf. Haac, "Deism in Marivaux."

6. There is an illustration showing the stage in Paul Gazagne, *Marivaux par Lui-Même,* p. 15.

Chapter Five

1. 1653-1743, Cardinal and chief advisor of Louis XV, virtual ruler of France 1726-43.

2. A ninth part appeared anonymously in 1739; a twelfth, also anonymous, in 1745; the latter was printed as a sequel to all editions until 1881. A more talented sequel by Madame Riccoboni (Marie-Jeanne Laboras de Mézières) was written in 1750; it appears in M as part twelve; Grimm thought it far superior to Marivaux' novel, but modern readers will not agree. Cf. M xcvi, c-cii, 581-82. A major revision in moral tones with a sequel, *The Virtuous Orphan* (1743) by Mary Mitchell Collyer, was reedited by McBurney and Shugrue

(Carbondale, Ill., 1965); it omits one-third of Marivaux and doubles the length of what remains; it is not a true translation, but it leads Marianne to an obvious and sentimental marriage with Valville.

3. M 285f, 295, 367f, 476, 527, all notes by Deloffre and his commentary in D, *Une Préciosité Nouvelle, Marivaux* pp. 441-42, and elsewhere.

4. Le Maître de Claville, *Traité du Vrai Mérite* (1734), 3rd ed. London, 1736, p. 403.

5. The novel was continued anonymously in 1756. Parts six to eight, reproduced in P, also in a German translation of 1753 and in an English version of 1765, cf. P xxvii-xxxi; as for *Marianne* (cf. note 2, above), the product is inferior.

6. Matucci, *Marivaux Narratore e Moralista* (Naples, 1958), p. 24.

7. E.g., the "reason of the heart" and the discussion of religion in the *Cabinet du Philosophe?* (p. 90), and the conceptions of evil and original sin, discussed below among the themes concerning society (p. 145). It has been noted that Marivaux is one of the authors about whom Rousseau has no unfavorable comment.

Chapter Six

1. G. Lanson, *op, cit.* in note 3, Chapter 4, pp. 26-28, and OD 667, n. 34.

Chapter Seven

1. Cf. Haac, "Marivaux and the *Honnête Homme"* and the glossaries in T II, M, P, and OD, by Deloffre.

2. Ruth Jamieson, *Marivaux, A Study in Sensibility*, p. 54, and Lester Crocker, *An Age of Crisis*, p. 418.

3. Cf. note 7, Chapter 5.

4. Marivaux is also a rationalist, cf. *L'Ile de la Raison*, but the reason proposed is a lesson in humility. He accepts the mysteries of faith unlike the deists who, like John Toland, saw Christianity "not mysterious," i.e., accessible to reason. Cf. note 5, Chapter 4. Compare Marivaux' idea of religion as half faith, half self-sacrifice with the irony of his early sponsor, Fontenelle, who says: One must give over only half of oneself to the kind of things one believes and preserve the other half to admit the contrary, if need be." (*Entretiens sur la Pluralité des Mondes,* ed. Calame, Paris: Didier, 1966; 3rd Evening, lines 21-24).

Selected Bibliography

Our abbreviations in the text refer to the *Oeuvres Complètes* and the Deloffre editions and Deloffre's *Marivaux et la Marivaudage;* the reference letters D, M, OD, OJ, P, T, and X appear in parentheses after the listing of the respective titles below.

Primary Sources

Dates of original editions are generally those of our *Chronology;* more exact indications are given in the critical editions by Deloffre where manuscript sources are also listed. Very few manuscripts remain.

1a. Complete Works:

Oeuvres Complètes de Marivaux. Paris: Veuve Duchesne, 1781. Vol. X (Ref: X) contains the complete *Homère Travesti* (only half in OJ); all other texts are available in the Deloffre editions.

2b. Critical Editions:

Marivaux, *Oeuvres de Jeunesse* (Ref: OJ), ed. Deloffre and Rigault, Paris: Gallimard, 1972.
Marivaux, *Journaux et Oeuvres Diverses* (Ref: OD), ed. Deloffre and Gillot. Paris: Garnier, 1969.
Marivaux, *Théâtre Complet* (Ref: T I, T II), ed. Deloffre. Paris: Garnier, 1968, vols. I and II.
Marivaux, *La Vie de Marianne* (Ref: M), ed. Deloffre. Paris: Garnier, 2nd ed., 1963.
Marivaux, *Le Paysan Parvenu* (Ref: P), ed. Deloffre. Paris: Garnier, 2nd ed., 1965.
Other critical editions with notable commentary (incorporated partly into those above): *Le Télémaque Travesti,* ed. Deloffre. Geneva: Droz, 1956; *Le Petit-Maître Corrigé,* ed. Deloffre. Geneva: Droz, 1955; *La Commère,* ed. Sylvie Chevalley. Paris: Hachette, 1966; *Le Miroir,* ed. Matucci. Naples: Ed. Scientifiche, 1958; cf. the latter's anthology, *Marivaux Narratore e Moralista, ibid.,* 1958.

3. Translations

Bentley, Eric, *The Classic Theatre*, IV: *Six French Plays*. Garden City: Doubleday Anchor Books, 1961. A good rendition of *Les Fausses Confidences*.

Conlon, Pierre and Lotte, *Marivaux, Two Plays*. Ontario: McAllister University Library, 1967. Good renditions of *La Double Inconstance, Les Fausses Confidences*.

Mandel, Oscar, *Seven Comedies by Marivaux, English by Oscar and Adrienne S. Mandel*. Ithaca: Cornell University Press, 1968. Renditions, partly faithful, partly fanciful, of *Arlequin Poli par l'Amour, La Double Inconstance, Le Triomphe de Plutus, Le Jeu, L'Heureux Stratagème, Les Fausses Confidences, L'Epreuve*.

Translations from Marivaux' time are listed in Séguin, J.A.R., *French Works in Translation*. Jersey City: Ross Paxton, 1966, for novels in vol. II (1731-40) and III (1741-50), for plays not rendered until 1762, in vol. V. Most were faithful but not one by Mary Collyer, cf. note 2, Chapter 5 above.

Secondary Sources

1a. Bibliographies of Marivaux Criticism

KLAPP, OTTO, *Bibliographic der französischen Literaturwissenschaft*. Frankfurt: Klostermann, since 1955, so far 9 vols., lists twenty-five or more contributions per year including four dissertations in 1970 for America alone.

For comments on critics, see Deloffre and Greene, below. Less complete are the bibliographies of Cioranescu, *Bibliographie de la Littérature Francaise du Dix-Huitième Siècle*. Paris: CNRS, 1969, and Rancoeur in *Revue d'Histoire Littéraire*, 6 times a year and annual.

2b. Books and Articles

D'ALEMBERT, *Eloge de Marivaux* in Marivaux, *Théâtre Complet*, ed. Dort. Paris: Le Seuil, 1964, pp. 17-28.

BONACCORSO, GIOVANNI, *Gli Anni Difficili di Marivaux*, Messina: Peloritana, 1965. The early years of Marivaux.

BRADY, VALENTINI PAPADOPOULOU, *Love in the Theater of Marivaux*. Geneva: Droz, 1970. Thematic analysis.

BROOKS, PETER, *The Novel of Wordliness*. Princeton: Princeton University Press, 1969. Sensitive study of *Marianne*.

COURVILLE, XAVIER DE, *Luigi Riccoboni, dit Lelio*. Vol. II,

Geneva: Droz, 1945; vol. III, Paris: Librairie *Théâtrale,* 1958. The Italian stage and its authors. Vol. I, Slatkine reprint 1967, with extensive bibliogr., lists, e.g., Riccoboni's editions of *Le Nouveau Théâtre Italien* and *Les Parodies du Nouveau Théâtre Italien* (I, 20-21).

COUTON, GEORGES, "Le Sieur Nicolas Carlet, Père de Pierre Carlet de Marivaux," *Revue d'Histoire Littéraire* 53: 92-94, 1953.

CROCKER, LESTER, *An Age of Crisis.* Baltimore: Johns Hopkins Press, 1959. Excellent panorama; attention given to novels.

——— "Portrait de l'Homme dans *Le Paysan Parvenu,*" *Studies on Voltaire 87: 253-76, 1972.*

DELOFFRE, FRÉDERIC, *Une Préciosité Nouvelle, Marivaux et le Marivaudage.* (Ref: D) Paris: A. Colin, 3rd ed. 1971. Basic study of language.

——— "Etat Présent des Etudes sur Marivaux," *Information Littéraire* 1964, pp. 191-99. Excellent résumé to be supplemented by the bibliography in D above and its 1967, 1971 supplements.

DESCOTES, MAURICE, *Les Grands Rôles du Théâtre de Marivaux.* Paris: Presses Universitaires, 1972. Theater study.

DESVIGNES-PARENT, LUCETTE, *Marivaux et l'Angleterre.* Paris: Klincksieck, 1970. Study of influences, actually often parallels.

——— "Plutarque et Marivaux," *Revue des Sciences Humaines* 124: 349-59, 1966.

——— "Marivaux et *Homère,*" *Revue d'Histoire Littéraire* 67: 529-36, 1967.

——— Survivance de la Pastyorale chez Marivaux," *French Studies* 22: 206-24, 1968.

DURRY, MARIE-JEANNE, *A Propos de Marivaux.* Paris: *Société* d'Enseignement *Supérieur,* 1960. Essential aspects of life and work.

ESPRIT CRÉATEUR (L'), I, no. 4, 1964, *Marivaux.*

FABRE, JEAN, "Marivaux," *Dictionnaire des Lettres Francaises; XVIIIe Siècle.* Paris: Arthème Fayard, 1960. II, 167-88. Excellent survey.

FRIEDRICHS, FRIEDHELM ALFRED, *Untersuchungen zur Handlungs und Vorgangsmotivik im Werke Marivaux'.* Diss. Heidelberg, 1965. Techniques and themes.

GAZAGNE, PAUL, *Marivaux par Lui-Même.* Paris: Le Seuil, 1964.

GILOT, MICHEL, "Maître Nicolas Carlet et son Fils, Marivaux," *Revue d'Histoire Littéraire* 68: 482-500, 1968. Important for biography.

——— "Quelques Traits du Visage de Marivaux," *ibid.,* 70: 391-99, 1970.

GREENE, E.J.H., *Marivaux*. Toronto: Toronto University Press, 1965. Important study; history of Marivaux criticism.

HAAC, OSCAR A., *"Marivaux and the Human Heart,"* Emory University Quarterly 12: 35-43, 1956.

——"Marivaux and the *Honnête Homme*," *Romanic Review* 50: 255-67, 1959.

—— "Humor through Paradox," *L'Esprit Créateur* I, 195-202, 1961.

—— "Paradox and Levels of Understanding in Marivaux," *Studies on Voltaire* 56: 693-707, 1967.

—— "Violence in Marivaux," *Kentucky Romance Quarterly* 14: 191-99, 1967.

—— "Deism in Marivaux, *Blictri* and Blectrue," *Romantic Review* 63: 5-19, 1972.

—— "Theories of Literary Criticism and Marivaux," *Studies on Voltaire* 88: 711-34, 1972.

JAMIESON, RUTH, *Marivaux, A Study in Sensibility*. New York: King's Crown Press, 1941; reprint: Octagon Books. Basic reinterpretation.

LAGRAVE, HENRI, *Marivaux et sa Fortune Littéraire*. Bordeaux: Ducros, 1970. Survey of reactions to Marivaux.

—— "Mahomet Second, Une Tragédie en Prose Inachevée de Marivaux," *Revue d'Histoire Littéraire* 71: 574-84, 1971. A discovery.

LARROUMET, GUSTAVE, *Marivaux, sa Vie et son Oeuvre*. Paris: Hachette, 1882. Essential reinterpretation.

LÜTHI, KATHY, *Les Femmes dans l'Oeuvre de Marivaux*. Bienne: Le Chandelier, 1943.

MCKEE, KENNETH, *The Theater of Marivaux*. New York: New York University Press, 1958. Useful study of plays and reactions to them.

MASON, HAYDN T. "Cruelty in Marivaux' Theater," *Modern Language Review* 62: 238-47, 1967. Interesting analysis.

MATUCCI, MARIO, *L'Opera Narrativa di Marivaux*. Naples: Pironti, 1962. The novels, with emphasis on the early work: important study.

—— "Su Alcuni Temi di Marivaux," *Studi in Onore di Vittorio Lugli*. Venice: Neri Pozza, 1967. On sensibility.

MAUZI, ROBERT, *L'Idée du Bonheur au Dix-Huitième Siècle*. Paris: A. Colin, 1960. Excellent section on Marivaux.

—— Preface to his edition of *Le Paysan Parvenu*, Paris 10/18, 1965.

MEYER, MARLYSE M. *La Convention dans le Théâtre d'Amour de Marivaux*. Sao Paulo: Ud. de Sao Paulo, 1961. Study of techniques.

MORHANGE, CLAUDE, *Les Jeunes Filles dans les Comédies de Marivaux.* Aix: Annales de la Faculté des Lettres, 1960.

MÜHLEMANN, SUZANNE, *Ombres et Lumières dans l'Oeuvre de Pierre de Carlet de Marivaux.* Berne: Herbert Lang, 1970. Suggestive study.

NELSON, ROBERT, *The Play within a Play.* New Haven: Yale University Press, 1958. Chapter on *Les Acteurs de Bonne Foi.*
——— "The Trials of Love in Marivaux' Theater," *University of Toronto Quarterly* 36: 237-48, 1967.

POULET, GEORGES, *Etudes sur le Temps Humain,* II, *La Distance Intérieure.* Paris: Plon, 1953. Existentialist view, cf. Spitzer.

RATERMANIS, J. B. *Etude sur le Comique dans le Théâtre de Marivaux.* Geneva: Droz, 1961.

RIGAULT, CLAUDE, *Les Domestiques dans le Théâtre de Marivaux.* Sherbrooke: Librairie de la Cité Universitaire, 1968.

ROUSSET, JEAN, *Forme et Signification.* Paris: J. Corti, 1964. Essential study of levels of meaning.

SCHAAD, HAROLD, *Le Thème de l'Etre et du Paraître dans l'Oeuvre de Marivaux.* Zurich: Juris, 1969. Themes, e.g., the mirror:

SHOWALTER, ENGLISH, *The Evolution of the French Novel, 1641-1782.* Princeton: Princeton University Press, 1972. Excellent survey.

SPITZER, LEO, "A Propos de *La Vie de Marianne,*" *Romantic Review* 44: 102-26, 1953. Answer to Poulet.

STEWART, PHILIP B., *Imitation and Illusion in the French Memoir Novel, 1700-1750.* New Haven: Yale University Press, 1969. Aspects of reality and realism, opposed to nineteenth-century techniques.

STACKELBERG, JÜRGEN, *Von Rabelais bis Voltaire.* Munich: C. H. Beck, 1970. Chapter on Marivaux' novels.
——— "Marivaux Narrateur," *Studi in Onore di Italo Siciliano.* Firenze: 1966, pp. 1155-63.

SWIDERSKI, MARIE LAURE, "La Pensée Sociale de Marivaux," *Revue de L'Université d'Ottawa* 41: 345-70, 1970. A balanced view.

Index